UNDER OPEN SKIES

UNDER OPEN SKIES

Mary S. Edgar

Toronto  1955

CLARKE, IRWIN & COMPANY LIMITED

Printed in Canada

To Campers Everywhere

FOREWORD

THESE short excerpts are taken from talks given in an out-door chapel at camp. The poems, in most cases, relate somewhat to the subjects of the talks. They are printed at the suggestion of my campers and counsellors, but are offered to campers everywhere in the hope they may be suggestive and helpful for their meditations "under open skies".

ACKNOWLEDGMENTS

Wherever possible, the quotations used in this book have been verified and their sources cited in foot notes. I am especially grateful to Mary L. Northway, Helen Ferguson Hastings, and Wilson MacDonald for permission to use their original poems in these pages. I wish here to acknowledge my indebtedness to them.

CONTENTS

Essays

xi

ESSAYS

CONTENTS

VERSES AND PRAYERS

xiii

UNDER OPEN SKIES

THE SENSE OF WONDER

NEAR my cabin, two small campers had obviously discovered something by the path to the lake. It was an unusual sight to see these ever-active nine-year-olds so motionless. I watched for a while from the window, then, out of curiosity, joined them. They were breathlessly watching a moth which had emerged from a drab grey chrysalis. Slowly the exquisite pale-green wings of a luna moth were unfolding and the delicate mauve spots were being revealed on its shining fragile wings. There was only hushed silence. A whistle sounded from the wharf for swimming, the juniors' most popular activity of the day, but neither of them paid the slightest attention. They were completely enthralled, for a miracle was happening before their wondering eyes.

Indeed, miracles *do* happen, and those who have the good fortune to spend much time in the out-of-doors will often discover in the ever-changing beauty of the days and nights some amazing thing which holds them spellbound. This sense of wonder is perhaps our most precious heritage. So closely akin is it to worship that in the presence of great beauty we often feel that we are standing on sacred ground, face to face with the great enigma of life.

> Flower in the crannied wall,
> I pluck you out of the crannies.
> I hold you here, root and all, in my hand,
> Little flower—but *if* I could understand
> What you are, root and all, and all in all,
> I should know what God and man is.[1]

The eternal question which the sense of wonder evokes can only be answered by the age-old words: "In the beginning *God*." As we meditate on those significant words and translate them for our own age, and our own selves, we exclaim in reverence, "Why, they mean God in the beginning, God *here* and *now*, and God on into the dim unknown future, God, the only explanation of the mystery and wonder of life."

Sometimes the question is asked, "How do I know there is a God if I cannot see Him?" Have you ever watched a mighty wind sweeping great waves with white caps up over the shore, bending the trunks of trees and tossing the branches about? You can never see the wind, but all around you can see what the wind is doing. God is like the wind. We cannot see Him, but everywhere we can see Him at work in His world. God is a Spirit, not confined, nor limited, nor restricted, but in all created

---

[1] Alfred, Lord Tennyson, "Flower in the Crannied Wall".

things. That means for us personally that He is in you and in me.

The name some of our Indian tribes use for God is "Gitche Manitou" or Great Spirit. When we use the name, "Great Spirit", we mean God, the ever-creating and ever-renewing Life in the universe. He is in the beauty and growth of the world about us, in the colour of the changing sunset, in the fragrance of the rose and the music of running water. He is in the mysterious migrating instinct of the birds, in the orderly movement of tides and stars, and in the structure and harmony of all created things.

An innate sense of wonder is something all children possess. Youth sometimes outgrows the thrill of surprise, or assumes a blasé attitude, while adults often lose completely the glory and lustre which wonder gives to life, and it becomes for them dull and monotonous. Yet there are many fortunate individuals who continue to experience all through their lives the adventure of living. They behold a universe so vast and amazing that the only possible response is an attitude of surprise and expectancy.

The scientists who delve deepest into the secrets of all life, from the vast planetary systems to the inner secrets of the atom, experience a deep sense of wonder, humility and reverence. We, however, often accept very casually electricity, television, radio, radar, jet propulsion, and atomic energy, failing to realize we are dealing with miracles, no less marvellous because they happen to belong to our own day and age. In the world our grandparents knew, these mysteries were too daring for dreams. God is constantly revealing the wonders of His universe, not only under open skies, but in the guarded laboratories among test tubes and electrons.

Let us guard, therefore, as a most precious heritage, our God-given sense of wonder. No day will then be commonplace, for we shall discover in it some unexpected aspect of beauty. No person will then be ordinary, for we shall catch a glimpse of a unique personality. No happening will then be unimportant, for we shall relate it to the amazing adventure of living. Wonder will keep us young in spirit, no matter what toll the years may take of health and strength, and wonder will keep us rich in appreciation, no matter what material possessions we may lose.

A Catalogue

This catalogue of lovely things
Is offered for perusal;
Not as treasures to be purchased,
But rather for infinite wonder,
That you may contemplate
The Artist Mind,
The Master of Dreams,
Who, with each Dawn,
Is ever bringing to birth
Beauty incomparable.

Consider these:
A sweep of sapphire lake,
With touches of white spray,
Set in a frame of birches.

The gossamer blue-green throats
Of humming birds, a-wing
Over the spikes of tall delphiniums.

An autumn day so amber clear
That every maple spreads
A tapestry of gorgeous red and gold.

The vivid shades of sunset,
Flaming first, fanfares of joy,
Then paling to a gentle lullaby.

A glowing fire beside a wooded shore,
With light reflected in the shining eyes
Of children, listening spell-bound to a tale.

A night bedecked with stars;
Spires of pointed spruce against the sky.
A far-off bugle sounding out "Good night!"

Only these few, from out the catalogue:
But turn the pages slowly;
Mountains, dawns, far islands,
Birds in flight, and jewelled waterfalls,
Quiet streams and waxen lily pads.
An endless index here!

All these are ours,
With added dividends
Of faith, adventure, joy;
And for the pure in heart
A passport to a Kingdom,
Where, the Eternal Wonder,
All-loving and all-wise,
Awaits the questing soul.

THE CHAPEL OF THE OUT-OF-DOORS

Enter the Temple Beautiful
The house not made with hands.
Rain-washed and green,
Wind-swept and clean
Beneath the blue it stands;
And no cathedral anywhere
Seemeth so holy or so fair.[1]

MANY campers are familiar with this poem for it is frequently used in outdoor Chapel services all across our land. So perfectly did it express the feelings of my own campers, that they arranged to have two verses etched on a bronze plaque, and later placed among the white birches at the entrance to the Chapel. Before it was hung, the plaque was taken to the poet, Virna Sheard, in her Toronto home. Her eyes lit up as she told of the occasion on which she wrote the poem. "The inspiration came to me in a dim cathedral-like forest of great Douglas firs on Vancouver Island. Every place of unspoiled beauty in God's great out-of-doors is to me a Temple Beautiful, a house not made with hands."

[1] Complete poem on pages 13, 14.

Clearly and unmistakably God, Himself, speaks to us through the wonder and the beauty of the growing things. On all sides is the amazing variety of His handiwork. Shakespeare reminds us that there are:

Books in the running brooks,
Sermons in stones, and good in everything.

When I was quite young I thought that other parts of the world could not possibly be as beautiful as my own land. Then the opportunity came for me to travel around the world for eleven months. I made many discoveries on that trip, not only about the people in the lands I visited, but about the amazing natural beauty of their mountains and waterfalls, their moonlit seas and tropical gardens.

One of these discoveries I made in Japan, on a walking trip to the Fuji Lake district, organized by the Tokyo Y.W.C.A., when we hiked with a group of over twenty high school girls. The spirit of adventure was strong and the girls were gay and carefree. We crossed lakes by boat, climbed mountain trails, and ate our lunches beside clear tumbling streams. At night we settled down, after the unique experience of a Japanese bath, in an inn where all the walls were sliding screens opening out onto a long balcony. Very early in the morning I was wakened by excited whispering: "Come out and see Mount Fuji!" I stepped out on the balcony, and saw two unforgettable pictures. The first was a long row of girls, in bright-coloured kimonos, standing silently at the edge of the gallery and gazing spell-bound at the glory of the sunrise, a breath-taking spectacle spread out before them. Then, behind the towering majesty of the cone-shaped sacred mountain of Japan, hung a crescent moon, in a sky tinged with the rose and gold of dawn. The crest of the mountain caught the crimson light and, down the long slopes, the red deepened into violet and purple. No one spoke. It was a moment for wonder and worship.

I returned from my travels sure, beyond all doubt, that God is impartial in His creating of beauty. He knows no international boundaries. On no special race does He bestow His lavish gifts of beauty. The whole world is the canvas on which He paints His masterpieces and in every land appreciative souls pause to look and marvel.

Some years ago I wrote a hymn for campers which begins with these words:

God who touchest earth with beauty.

The whole earth, and not a favoured part, has been touched with beauty, and there are people of every land who respond to the evidence of God's love. The realization grows within us that a universal love encompasses the whole world, and it becomes a natural response to whisper reverently, "*Our Father*".

From the earliest dawn of the centuries men everywhere have glimpsed God through His handiwork; wonder and worship have been the instinctive response. The first altars were built under open skies. The Persian sunworshippers beheld a semblance of God's glory in the rising sun. The Eastern seers studied the stars and followed one special star to Bethlehem. Jesus told His incomparable stories of a loving Father by a lake shore and on the hillsides. The underlying message in many of His wonderful stories is in the simple words, "When ye pray, say Our Father." Whether we worship God under open skies or turn to Him under Gothic roofs, we know that the whole universe is His "Temple Beautiful".

No need for wordy sermons
    Beneath these open skies,
Where everything about us
    Reveals some fresh surprise:
Where every glimpse of beauty,
    Sky, forest, lake and sod,
Proclaims a timeless message
    Of the handiwork of God.

The Temple Beautiful

*Enter the Temple Beautiful,
The house not made with hands.
Rain-washed and green,
Wind-swept and clean
Beneath the blue it stands;
And no cathedral anywhere
Seemeth so holy or so fair.

It hath no heavy gabled roof,
No door with lock and key;
No window bars
Shut out the stars,
Its aisles are wide and free.
Here through the night each altar light
Is but a moonbeam silver white.

Silently as the temple grew
At Solomon's command,
Still as things seem
Within a dream
This rose from out the land,
And all the pillars grey and high
Lifted their arches to the sky.

Here in the perfume of the leaves,
The incense of the pines,

13

The magic scent
That has been pent
Within the tangled vines.
No censer filled with spices rare,
E'er swung such sweetness on the air.

*And all the golden gloom of it
Holdeth no haunting fear,
For it is blest and giveth rest
To those who enter here.
Here in the evening who shall know
But God, Himself, walks to and fro.

And music past all mastering
Within the chancel rings.
None could desire
A sweeter choir
Than that which soars and sings
Till far the scented shadows creep
And quiet darkness bringeth sleep.

Virna Sheard

* Inscribed on a Chapel plaque.

"CONSIDER THE LILIES"

TO the boy, Jesus, a flaming red lily once whispered a wonderful secret. Had He not been a person with seeing eyes and listening ears, He might have missed the message, but He was wide-eyed and alert and sensitive.

He loved the fields and the hills around the little town of Nazareth. But, as Jesus was a helper in the little carpenter shop of the village, it was seldom He could take time to wander off alone or with His friends to enjoy the open spaces.

On the long work bench and about the shop were ploughs to be mended, yokes to be fixed, cart wheels to be repaired and beds to be restrung with rope. Day after day He worked away among the fragrant shavings of cedar and sandalwood. These tasks demanded His attention. But there were occasions when He could design and create something Himself, and He found it a joy to whittle and plane and bring out the beautiful natural grain of the wood.

He was particularly interested in the people who came in and out of the work shop. Some were kind, considerate and generous; others were sullen, impatient and stingy. Some worried about money, taxes, and the future. Others, burdened with fears, had forgotten how to laugh. Among the children who played about the doorway some were gay and gentle, but there were also selfish, quarrelsome ones, insensitive to the hurts they inflicted. He often pondered these things in His heart.

One beautiful summer day He slipped off to His beloved hills to enjoy the quiet and the beauty of the valleys and the skies. These out-of-door expeditions always brought joy and gladness and serenity. The beauty of the world spoke to Him so clearly of God, of God, His Heavenly Father. He was happy in this sense of trust and confidence and love. Suddenly He remembered "those others", neighbours and friends with all their worries and fears. His own spirits were weighed down with a realization of their anxieties and doubts.

Beside Him, where He sat on the hillside, were hundreds of red lilies scattered among the stones and the grass. Bending over to study the beauty of the flowers, He thought to Himself that even Solomon, the King, in all his glory could never have been arrayed in such beauty. Then it was that an amazing thing happened. As He held one of the lilies in His hand it seemed to whisper a message. It seemed to say to Him that it was a loving God who clothed the flowers in such gorgeous colours and just as certainly would a loving God meet the needs of all His children.

Jesus never forgot that message. Years later when a group of His disciples were troubled and anxious about the future, He again picked one of those little red flowers and, holding it in His hand, he said, "Consider the lilies." He shared with them His profound belief that God who clothes the wayside flowers with beauty, and protects the little birds from harm, would also take them into His care and keeping, for each one of them was a child of the Father. He taught them the secret of the flower, that what they needed most was trust in their Heavenly Father.

> Jesus, the poet of Galilee,
> Sang that the weary might be free;
> Sang of the lilies—how their glory
> Shamed the best at a king's command
> Sang His truths in a lyric story,
> Even the poor could understand.[1]

We live in an age of fear. The future is full of perplexities for us as it was for that little group of troubled disciples. We, too, worry about material things, food and clothes, and lose our sense of perspective for the things that are of more lasting value. Jesus would remind us that the essentials for daily living are the concern of our Heavenly Father, and that He is able to supply the needs of His children.

The stress and strain of our modern age comes from the fact that the times have changed and our needs are

[1] Wilson MacDonald

no longer simple. We consider as essentials a great excess of luxuries and all the "extras". Could we but learn to say a grace for the simple gifts of God, such as water and food and health and sunshine, we would come nearer to the thinking of Jesus and would undoubtedly be much happier.

If we would take time off occasionally to climb a hillside, our little world of affairs, with its problems and perplexities, would be seen from the heights in a truer perspective. We, too, would find it well worth while to "consider the lilies", or the so-called common flowers of the fields, the white daisies, the golden buttercups, and the fragrant pink clover. We would realize with what a lavish hand and an artist's sense of beauty the great Creator enriches and glorifies His world with colour, song and fragrance. The slogan the commercial florists offer to those who would express their love and sympathy to friends is the oft-heard phrase, "Say it with flowers." How clearly and persistently God announces His love each new day as the dewy meadows and hillsides are sprinkled with fresh blossoms for our enjoyment and our comfort.

Consider These

When the Boy of Nazareth, long ago,
Climbed the hills where the lilies grow,
He learned from the flowers the mystery
Of a Father's love, so full and free.

Joyously His message then
He gave to the troubled hearts of men:
"Fear not. Your loving Father sees
Your smallest need. Consider these!"

Consider too each goodly thing,—
The flaming Dawn, returning Spring,
And stars that faithful vigil keep
Above His children fast asleep.

Water, cool and crystal clear,
Sunshine with its warmth and cheer,
Food and drink that give delight
To every healthy appetite.

Beyond computing is the love
Showered on us from above.
O may we then the Giver please,
And graciously "consider these".

Meditation Out of Doors

It is good for tired nerves
To sit quietly
In a place of refreshing beauty.

It is healing for the soul
To let the eyes wander
Unhurriedly over a broadloom of grass.

It is inspiration for the spirit
To look at blue sky
Through a canopy of pine trees.

It is peace for the whole being
To rest silently
And wait for an unspoken word.

THE CHALLENGE OF MOUNT EVEREST

O N the eve of her Coronation Day, the young Queen
Elizabeth was wakened from her sleep to hear an
announcement: "Two members of Sir John Hunt's expedition have reached the top of Mount Everest." Why
should the Queen have been wakened to hear that news?
She had retired early the night of June first, realizing that
the most important day of her life lay before her. She
had said in a message, broadcast before the coronation,
"I ask you, whatever your religion may be, to pray for me
on that day,—to pray that God may give me wisdom and
strength to carry out the solemn promises I shall be making, that I may faithfully serve Him, and you, all the days
of my life." It was to be a demanding day, a day of
pomp and splendour, during which she would be watched
and photographed and televised for millions; but it was to
be also a day of self-consecration to life-long service.

A new Elizabethan age was beginning! Sir Winston
Churchill had said in one of his speeches, "Famous have
been the reigns of our queens. Some of the greatest
periods of history have unfolded under their sceptre."
That the peak of the highest mountain in all the world

should be reached on the eve of her coronation might well be the worthy symbol of a new Elizabethan age of dreams and daring and achievement.

Let us think of the achievement of those two daring young men, Edmund Hillary, an Australian beekeeper, and Tenzing, an Indian guide, born in the mountains of Nepal. There had been many unsuccessful attempts to conquer Mount Everest. Seven well-organized British attempts and two Swiss attempts, dating over the past thirty-five years, had all failed to reach the top. The motto of the latest expedition was, "One for all and all for one." Colonel Sir John Hunt, the leader of the expedition, an older man than his companions, knew that he would not be the one to reach the top, but he carried the pack sacks to heights as high as it was possible for him to climb, choosing the heaviest ones. It was marvellous team work that won final success.

Hillary, telling the story of the last desperate efforts, said: "We had reached the foot of the most formidable vertical rock step. We had seen this through our binoculars from far away and realized that at this altitude (over twenty-eight thousand feet) it might spell the difference between success and failure. The rock was smooth and almost holdless. One possibility of tackling it remained. There was a great cornice on one side and a narrow crack between the cornice and the rock, (a twelve-thousand-foot drop below). I moved into this crack and

22

kicking backwards with my crampons (spiked boots), I gained a purchase on the frozen snow behind me and inched backward and upward with a fervent prayer that the cornice would remain attached to the rock. Progress was slow. Tenzing paid out the rope and I was finally over the top of the rock. I lay still, regaining my breath. Then for the first time I felt that nothing now could keep us from reaching the top. When I recovered, I took a firm stance and commenced towing in the rope as Tenzing wiggled up. We still had no idea where the top was. As we cut around one hump, another higher one swung into view. At last I realized the ridge, instead of rising, now dropped sharply away and far below were landmarks we knew. We stood on the summit! We shook hands. Then casting Anglo-Saxon formalities aside, Tenzing threw his arms around my shoulders and we thumped each other on the back."[1]

As quickly as weary, happy men could descend the steep slopes, as fast as excited Indian guides could carry the news down the lower Himalayas, as speedily as relays of runners could carry the message through steaming jungles, and as miraculously as news can now flash over continents and oceans, the word reached London, and a young Queen was given the thrilling message. Edmund Hillary has been knighted and the Indian guide has trav-

[1] From *The Ascent of Everest* by Sir John Hunt, published and copyrighted by Hodder & Stoughton Ltd., London.

elled from his mountain home to Buckingham Palace to receive from the Queen's own hands the George Medal.

On her twenty-first birthday Queen Elizabeth broadcast from South Africa a challenge to the youth of the Commonwealth. She said: "In the presence of you all, I make a solemn vow to you, that I will devote my whole life, whether it be long or short, to the service of my people. I shall not have the strength to carry out this resolution alone, unless you join with me in it, as I now invite you to do. God help me to make good my vow, and God bless all of you who are willing to share it."

Like those who aspired to conquer Mount Everest's high and lonely peak, our Queen envisions a lofty goal. She has made a vow to give her best throughout her life. No peak in life could be higher or more difficult than that. She challenges us to join with her in giving our best in service to our own day and age. What would it mean if we accepted this challenge? It could mean, if there were enough of us, a new and glorious Elizabethan age, the golden age of which prophets and poets have dreamed.

"The best of each for the good of all." This is the pledge many campers make as they place their faggots on the first fire of the Council Ring. Our *best* will always be our Mount Everest. There can be nothing higher! Dare we accept the challenge of setting forth toward the goal of our best? Only will it be possible for us to suc-

24

ceed if we, too, humbly add: "God help me to make good my vow!"

> Just as I am, young, strong and free
> To be the best that I can be;
> For truth and righteousness, and Thee
> Lord of my life, I come.[1]

[1] Marianne Farningham.

To Youth

You who are young and eager
    Have mountains ahead to scale;
Though the slopes be steep and lonely
    'Tis not in your heart to fail.
With faith in the unknown future,
    And valour to meet each test,
In a spirit of high adventure
    Gain the heights of your *best*.

You who are young and a dreamer
    Will glimpse a city to build,
Where the shining towers of justice
    Will rise as you have willed.
Work must be ever the key-stone
    To make a dream come true
And a building greatly needed
    May arise because of you.

You who are young and daring
    Must help the prayers come true,
Of a world with deep forebodings
    And needing the faith of you;
Needing the strong true vision
    Of a day when war shall cease,
When the atom re-employed
    Shall build the bridge of peace.

SUNSETS

THERE was an unusually magnificent sunset on a recent summer evening. Across the lake the crescent moon was making a shining pathway, and a rippled edge of silver was curving on the white sand beach. In the west, gorgeous colours were blending into soft pastel shades, their loveliness reflected in the still waters of the lake. It was a scene of breath-taking beauty, yet it came unannounced. Earlier in the summer the eclipse of the sun had been headlined in the newspapers for weeks. Astronomers and scientists had travelled to many far parts of the world to watch the brief phenomenon of a shadowed sun. Here was a spectacle of unrivalled glory; yet only a few campers paused in their play and stood at the edge of the shore to watch it.

Suppose the sun went down like that in a flame of glory only once every fifty years. What a world-wide flurry of excitement there would be! Scientists and astronomers would be out of doors on hilltops to study it; artists would be ready with their canvases set up; television technicians would be on hand to record the whole pageant of beauty for the "shut-ins", and radios would give a breathless minute-by-minute description for the blind. If you were too young to have seen it yourself, your parents would tell you about it and you would exclaim wistfully, "Oh, I *do* hope I'll live to see a sunset!"

Or suppose you had to pay to see a sunset. If some enterprising super-showman could curtain off the western world and advertise: "The Greatest Show on Earth. A different pageant with new colours every evening. Reserved seats two dollars, standing room twenty-five cents." What a scramble there would be to get in! People would ask each other, "Which sunset did you see this season?", just as they ask which opera or picture or ballet have you seen.

Almost every evening it is possible to watch a sunset without any ticket of admission, and no two sunsets are ever alike. The only price you have to pay is to pause in the rush of the day's busy activity and be still for a few moments and watch. More than a hundred years ago Sir Walter Scott wrote a short poem "On the Setting Sun". The message of this poem is as timely as today's sunset.

> Those evening clouds, that setting ray
> And beauteous tints, serve to display
>   Their great Creator's praise;
> Then let the short-lived thing call'd man,
> Whose life's comprised within a span,
>   To Him his homage raise.
> We often praise the evening clouds,
>   And tints so gay and bold,

But seldom think upon our God,
  Who tinged these clouds with gold.

The mystery and beauty of a flaming sunset is not only a delight to the eye, but it seems to lift our spirits out of the humdrum round of the day's activity into a rarefied atmosphere of wonder and worship. As a call to prayer, a sunset comes sometimes like a gentle sanctus bell, in soft shades of rose and violet, sometimes like a trumpet call, with unfurled banners of gold and crimson. Whether the colours are unfolded in soft tones or brilliant shades, a beautiful sunset comes as a benediction and an inspiration.

Often I heard in the East the clear sound of the muezzin's call to prayer from the Mohammedan mosques. Five times every twenty-four hours the call goes forth from the slender minarets silhouetted against the sky. All activities stop and the faithful bow low in prayer to Allah, wherever they happen to be. In the midst of the jostle of a busy city street or out on the dusty roads, they acknowledge the reality of God.

A gorgeous sunset could be for us a muezzin's call to prayer, a pause to remember "There is no God but God", and to whisper a deep-felt thanks for the splendour of the evening skies. A Divine Voice calls often from the minarets of silence, "Be still and know that I am God."

To *be still* is the price of admission into many wonderful visions and experiences. So much of beauty and inspiration is missed in the hectic rush of our daily living, whereas there are treasures beyond price available for those who are willing to pause and look and listen. Living in the out-of-doors presents many opportunities to get away into the silence and solitude of shore and woods. Short intervals of escape, even from one's friends, will give inner resources of poise and confidence. Choose, therefore, a beautiful sunset as a special occasion to bathe your soul in beauty.

> What is this life if, full of care,
> We have no time to stand and stare?[1]

[1] William Henry Davies, "Leisure".

The Sunset

When I was a little child,
　　My mother used to say,
"Come and look at the sunset!"
　　And I would turn from play,
To stand and watch in wonder
　　Till the colours died away.

The wealth of a thousand sunsets
　　Through life have added their gold;
Every day has been enriched,
　　When I've watched the shades unfold.
Never by poem nor painting
　　Could such beauty rare be told.

For the glory of the western skies,
　　We never can repay,
But we can show our gratitude,
　　When at the close of day,
We lift our eyes to wonder,
　　And lift our hearts to pray.

OIL FOR OUR LAMPS

JESUS was a master of the art of story-telling. Centuries ago He told His stories, under open skies, on hilltops and by the shores of Galilee. His stories made a deep impression on those who heard them. For many years they were not written down but were told and retold. Eventually His stories and His messages were collected in what we call the Gospels, to be made known to all the world.

One story, especially for girls, is known as "The Wise and Foolish Virgins". It tells of what took place at a wedding when ten girls were in attendance as bridesmaids.

An Eastern wedding, even to this day, in China, or India or Palestine, can be almost as spectacular as a "Santa Claus Parade", especially if the bride belongs to a socially important family. A Chinese wedding procession through the streets of the ancient city of Peking stands out in my memory as a never-to-be-forgotten pageant.

The bride, in the story of Jesus, had chosen her closest friends as bridesmaids. They had a significant part to play. It was to be a night wedding with a gaily-lighted

32

procession through the city streets from the house of the bride to the home of the groom. To the bridesmaids went the honour of carrying beautiful brass lamps on either side of the bride to light her way. In the East it is also customary to have numerous paid musicians and liveried servants to carry, with great display, the wedding gifts. The streets were lined with crowds of interested people, friends of the wedding party, and of the curious who always love to watch a procession.

We can imagine how thrilled the bridesmaids must have been. They would naturally plan with enthusiasm the gowns and the jewels they would wear, and their lamps would be polished until they shone like gold. Then, waiting eagerly for the moment when the groom would come for his bride, they all lighted their lamps. To the horror of everyone, five lights flickered and went out. In desperation five panic-stricken girls tried to borrow oil from the others. They cried, "Give us of your oil for our lamps have gone out!" But the others answered, "Not so, for we have not enough for both of us. Go to the merchants who sell oil and buy for yourselves." In mad haste they rushed off to buy oil. In the meantime the bridegroom arrived with his gay and colourful retinue and the procession moved on through the streets without them.

Bitter was the disappointment of the young bride. She had counted on ten of her friends, but five of them

33

had "let her down". It was not only a personal disappointment, but a matter of chagrin for the groom, the parents, the friends and the spectators who lined the streets. When finally the procession reached the home of the groom, the party entered through the gateway for the marriage ceremony, the feast, and the music. The door was closed.

At last came the breathless five, but they were too late. They knocked on the door, but the message sent to them by the groom was, "I know you not!"

When Jesus told this story to those girls of long ago, what was the message He wanted to convey? His stories have a timeless message and we might ask, what is the meaning for girls today? Had He discovered from His observations that many girls thought so much about themselves, their own pleasures, their own appearance, and their own interests, that they had no inner resources to meet the responsibilities Youth must face? They had no oil for their lamps.

The other five were as attractive and as popular, but different in one respect. They could be depended on, for they had a sense of responsibility. They did not fail their friend. They had oil to meet the demands of the situation.

What is this "oil", or its equivalent in life? It is character, a spiritual force within which each of us must shape for ourselves. It cannot be borrowed, bought, or

34

made available at a moment's notice. Life will bring to each of us many obligations for which we must be prepared.

The One who told this story is, Himself, "The Light of the World". He can give us "oil for our lamps". He can help us to acquire those inner resources of character, the marks of which are loyalty, dependability, and loving service.

His Lamps

His lamps are we, to shine where He has need.
Our light may be the only gleam to lead
Some faltering one along an upward trail:
Without our lamp a groping one may fail.

Choose we then, as our first and highest aim
To hold aloft a clear and steady flame,
That we may know when Life's adventure ends
We have not been unworthy of our friends.

"WHEN I CONSIDER THE HEAVENS"

TO sleep out under the stars for the first time, on a clear summer night, is a memorable experience. You snuggle down in your bed roll, the last flickering embers of the camp fire gradually die down, and your camp friends finally stop talking. Suddenly you become vividly aware of the dark canopy overhead, studded with innumerable stars. Never before has the immensity of the universe appeared so impressive. As you lie awake in the silence and beauty of the night, alone with your thoughts, a feeling of awe and wonder comes over you. A deep sense of the presence of God rises within you, and there is a new consciousness of the immanence of God in the world about you.

Long ago, a shepherd lad who watched his flocks night after night on the hills of Palestine was also impressed by the glory of the heavens. In the matchless songs which are still treasured as the Psalms of David, he gave expression to his feelings. Thus sang the young poet:

> The heavens declare the glory of God,
> And the firmament showeth His handiwork.[1]

[1] *Psalms*, xix, I

> What is man, that Thou are mindful of him
> And the son of man, that Thou visitest him?[1]

It seemed to David almost unbelievable that God, who created so vast and wonderful a world, concerned Himself with man. Yet as he thought through this mystery, the conviction grew that God was more than the impersonal creator of the stars. He was One who was ever mindful of His children, fashioned as they were in His image and endowed with His spirit.

> Thou . . . hast crowned him with glory and honour
> Thou madest him to have dominion over the works
> of Thy hands.[2]

The vastness of the heavens was something David marvelled over, yet he never dreamed of the immensity of the universe as it has been made known to us in our day. Astronomers who have explored with their telescopes the infinite reaches of space, have given us facts and figures which are staggering.

The planet on which we live is only one of the satellites of the sun, from which we are ninety million miles distant. Its light, travelling at 186,000 miles a second, comes to us in eight minutes, and the heat from the sun makes life possible on our planet. Yet there are other satellites of the sun, Saturn, Jupiter and Uranus, which are so far distant that heat does not reach them at all.

[1] *Psalms*, viii, 4
[2] *Psalms*, viii, 5-6

In David's time the sun was considered the centre of the universe. Now we know it is but a speck of a star among millions of stars in our galaxy, the main constellations of which may be seen in the milky way. Even Arcturus, the reddish star which can easily be located in line with the crooked handle of the dipper is a thousand times larger than our sun. Hercules is a constellation much greater than the group of stars about our sun, with fifty thousand or more stars, and so far away that the light we faintly see tonight started to travel toward us thirty-four thousand years ago. Beyond our galaxy which includes all the stars with which we are familiar are vast numbers of galaxies so far away that they appear as dim nebulous clouds. Beyond the constellation of Andromeda, faintly visible on a clear night, is an egg-shaped nebula which we are told is a grouping of many millions of stars seen from a distance of more than a million light years. It is beyond human comprehension to grasp the distances which are indicated by the world's largest telescope on Palomar in California.

With our appreciation of the immensity of space we, too, like David, experience a deeper awareness of God as the Creator. We also experience a deeper sense of wonder that He, who is Omnipotent, is also mindful of His children. Jesus, however, was the One who most fully glimpsed the truth, that God is not only the great Reality and Creative Spirit in and through His world,

39

but is "Our Father". Momentous and poignant was His conviction that there is a tender and eternal relationship between God and His children.

> Whoso draws nigh to God one step
>   Through doubtings dim,
> God will advance the miles
>   In blazing light to him.

The camper, tucked in a bed roll, under the stars, marvelling over the mystery of the universe, the immensity of space, and his or her part in the great plan of life, finds comfort in remembering the evening benediction of Taps, which nightly sends its bugle-clear notes across the lake and the hills and the sky.

> Day is done,
> Gone the sun,
> From the lake
> From the hills
> From the sky.
> All is well
> Safely rest
> God is nigh.

Taps

Day is done,
Gone the sun,

    Clear, through the gathering dusk, a bugle sounds,
        In quick response the campers turn from play;
    While through the silent hills the call resounds,
        They stand erect to honour close of day.

From the lake,
From the hills,
From the sky.

    From western skies the colours slowly die,
        The stars above the pines their watches keep.
    Another joyous day goes swiftly by,
        Another night bestows her gift of sleep.

All is well,
Safely rest,

    A treasure-trove, life in the open brings,
        Of magic gifts to hold for years to be.
    Adventure, laughter, friends,—all goodly things,
        And lessons learned from flower, bird and tree.

    A sense of genuine pride in work well done,
        A strength of body and a glowing tan.
    Joy of achievement in a skill new-won,
        Assurance "all is well" in life's great plan.

God is nigh.

As 'neath the stars the echoes softly fade,
An over-ruling sense of peace is there.
Since "God is nigh", no need to be afraid.
He hears the faintest whisper of a prayer.

A LEGACY OF JEWELS

IN the fairy tales of our childhood, the appearance of the old god-mother brought a touch of magic, for concealed under her cloak were incredible gifts for the little princess. In these fanciful tales there is an element of truth and symbolism. Each of us at birth has been endowed with rare gifts which could be likened to precious stones. Not realizing how priceless the endowment is, however, we fail to cherish it or even to guard it with care. Only when we lose one of these precious gifts do we begin to understand its worth.

The first precious stone is a glowing, radiant gem, the ruby of health. Health puts a sparkle in your eyes, a glow in your cheeks, and gives you animation and vitality for the many and varied activities in which you find enjoyment. We take health as a matter of fact, and what a catastrophe it is to lose this incomparable good gift. If we close our eyes for a few moments, and think how terrible it would be, never to be able to open them again on the familiar world around us, we more fully understand the bitter tragedy of blindness. There are countless wheel-chair people, children on crutches, and victims of a great variety of afflictions, who will never be able to enjoy the free, happy out-door life which is ours. The ruby of health is a treasure beyond price. Do you value it? Do you remember to say a grace sometimes for sight, and hearing, and straight, strong legs and a good heart?

The emerald in your treasure chest is the out-door world which is yours to know and to enjoy, with all its beauty of fields and forests, lakes and streams. Your gift, as campers, is a particularly glowing gem. Countless millions of people live in crowded cities, work at noisy machines, and sleep in stuffy rooms. Many of them have never camped by a blue lake, followed paths through the forests, or slept under the stars. "Spring Fever" expresses a fourteen-year-old factory girl's longing for the out-of-doors.

> I want to get out in the country
>   Away from the dust and the grime,
> And wrap my arms round a crooked tree
>   And climb, and climb, and climb.
>
> I want to get out by a wide blue lake
>   Where the world and the sky are big,
> And fill my hands with the clean warm sand
>   And dig, and dig, and dig.
>
> I want to get out in an open place
>   Where I can see the sun,
> And breathe the pine-tree scented air
>   And run, and run, and run.

44

I want to climb a high steep hill
And find a bubbling spring,
And lift my arms to the God of Life
And sing, and sing, and sing.

I want to get out in a forest cool
Oh far, and far away,
And kneel beside a purple pool
And pray, and pray, and pray.

The pearl, a gleaming white gem with an exquisite lustre, is the gift of purity, one of the loveliest things in a growing girl.

Like Thy springs and running water
Make me crystal pure.

Reverence for yourself, as a unique person, will make it possible for you to discriminate between the cheap and tawdry things, and those that are true and pure and of lasting worth.

I have to live with myself, and so
I must be fit for myself to know.

Your own honest judgement, and the wise guidance of older people whom you love and respect, will help you, as you grow up, to pass confidently through the new and perplexing experiences of adolescence, into the greater responsibilities of womanhood. Purity is truly a "pearl of great price".

45

The sapphire, deep blue as the evening skies, represents character-in-the-making,—the potential You. All gems are originally "in the rough" and must be ground and polished to bring out their brilliance and intrinsic worth. So, too, the shaping of character and the development of all one's innate talents requires work, discipline, and self-control. Sincerity and dependability are essentials in a life that is worth while.

Blue stands for all that is tested and true.

The diamond, most precious of all gems, represents the gift of life itself. Time is the material out of which life is made, and to each of us is given our allotment of days and years. An old quotation comes to mind: "Lost somewhere between sunrise and sunset, a golden hour, set with sixty diamond minutes. No reward is offered, for it can never be returned."

Of time, we can only possess today. Tomorrow is a hope and yesterday is a memory. In the words from the ancient Sanscrit:

But today well-lived, makes every yesterday
A dream of happiness
And every tomorrow a vision of hope.
Look well, therefore, to this day.
Such is the salutation of the dawn!

Time is more precious than diamonds, for with all the wealth of the world, we could never buy an extra day of life, nor re-live an hour that is gone. Solomon, one of the wisest men of old, left us this little prayer:

> So teach us to number our days
> That we may apply our hearts unto wisdom.

God grant that we may guard well these precious jewels entrusted to our care: the ruby of health, the emerald of beauty, the pearl of purity, the sapphire of sincerity and the diamond of life, so that when our allotment of time is ended, the world will be a better, happier place because we lived and gave of our best.

My Purpose

To guard my health
    And keep my body fair
That I may stronger be
    To do and dare.

To keep my mind
    Unsullied, glad and free
That Truth and Beauty
    May abide with me.

To be a friend
    And prove from day to day
Sincere and kind
    At home, at work, at play.

To follow always upward
    Life's high quest,
And find through knowing Christ
    My very best.

PLAYING THE GAME

THE Fifth British Empire and Commonwealth Games opened in Vancouver with twenty-two competing nations and the usual colourful pageantry. The captain of the Canadian team at the official opening pronounced on behalf of all competing athletes: "We declare that we will take part in the spirit of true sportsmanship."

What are the qualities of true sportsmanship that are essentials also in the greatest game of all, the game of Life? We might list them under five headings:

Fair Play

This means playing the game honestly and fairly, never taking an unfair advantage over others, and, in other words, following the golden rule: "Do unto others as you would that they do unto you."

Team Work

No game can be played alone. Since we must play with others, there must be a give and take. The player who hangs on to the ball or puck instead of passing it

49

has not learned team work. It is necessary to pull to-gether.

Graceful Winning

This means accepting success without having it turn our heads. We never win entirely by our own efforts. Many people contribute to our success; therefore it is fit-ting that we should be modest.

Gallant Losing

We cannot always win. To accept defeat gallantly is evidence of a fine spirit.

Never-say-die Spirit

Many an athlete loses because he gives up too soon. He should be able to keep up a steady persistence through to the last minute of play. Many a player wins because he gives all he has till the final whistle blows.

On board ship with a delegation to the Olympic games was a girl, popular and attractive, and, of course, "tops" in her particular sport. All were following a strict régime of training on board,—strenuous days of exercising, care-ful dieting and early-to-bed hours. One night this girl attended a very gay, late party given in her honour by a wealthy passenger. The committee member who dis-

50

covered her there suggested tactfully that it would be wise to go below. To this advice she said, "Oh, don't worry! I can take it!" Next day the committee met and her name was reluctantly removed from the list of contestants.

The game of Life calls for training, discipline, and self-control. There are many standards of behaviour not good enough. We may think we can "get away with it", but not if we would hold our place on the team.

> We can't all play a winning game,
>   Someone is sure to lose,
> Yet we can play, so that our name
>   No one dare abuse;
> That when the Master Referee
>   Scores against our name,
> It won't be whether we won or lost,
>   But how we played the game.[1]

Jesus was the supreme example of One who was Victor in the game of Life. He won no crown of laurel, but a crown of thorns. Nevertheless, for all time, He is the shining example of One who played the game of Life by every rule of good sportsmanship.

> One who never turned His back
> But marched breast forward.

Life's greatest reward for any of us would be to hear from the Master Referee words of approbation: "Well done. You have played the game!"

[1] J. B. Downie

51

Team Play

Not chosen to play?
    Why of course you were!
Your team is called,
    And you're needed there.

In the game of Life
    Each one takes part,
We have no sub,
    Nor counterpart.

We abide by rules
    And play it fair;
As part of the team
    One aim we share.

The grind of training
    We dare not shirk,
For success is ours,
    As the fruit of work.

When the whistle blows
    And the game is done,
Perhaps we've lost,
    Or perhaps we've won.

The thing that matters
    Most will be,
If a Voice within
    Breathes: "Victory!"

FINDING THE BLUEBIRD

ONE of the greatest allegories of our age, beautiful in its symbolism, is *The Bluebird*, a fairy play by Maeterlinck. With a poetical mysticism, it tells the story of the quest for happiness.

Two children, Tyltyl, a ten-year-old boy and Mytyl, a six-year-old sister, lived in a woodcutter's cottage on the edge of a great forest. It was Christmas Eve and from their windows they could see a gaily-lighted tree and a happy party in the grand house across the road. Since they did not expect Father Christmas to visit their poor home, they were playing a game of "Pretend", when suddenly an old woman entered, obviously a fairy in disguise. "Have you the bird that is blue?" she asked. But Tyltyl had only a little grey dove in a cage. "It is not blue enough," said the old woman. "You will have to go and find the one I want for my little girl, who is ill. The Bluebird will bring happiness." Then the fairy gave the children a mysterious little hat with a shining diamond on it, and explained that by pressing the top they could see "the Soul of things"; if they gave it a little turn to the right, they would discover the Past, and if they turned it to the left, they would behold the Future.

53

With the fairy's cap they watched a magic transformation taking place. The old woman turned into a young and beautiful princess; the bare little cottage sparkled and shone; the common everyday things, Bread, Fire, Water, Milk, even Cat and Dog, appeared as marvellous creatures. But most wonderful of all was Light, who appeared in surpassing loveliness, draped in shimmering veils.

As they set forth on the quest for the Bluebird of Happiness, with Light as guide, they were accompanied by these familiar friends. The story tells of the many strange and beautiful places they visited on their journey.

They passed over the threshold of the Land of Memory, where they found their dear old grandparents whom they had almost forgotten. They searched the fantastic Palace of Night, where they saw and heard much that was wonderful, but found no Bluebird. Under the guidance of Light, they visited the Kingdom of the Future, and a dazzling azure palace where they saw the little children who are waiting to be born. Time, an old man with an hour-glass, starts the unborn children off in a magnificent golden galley with white sails.

Then all alone, while their companions waited at the gateway, the children, with great apprehension, continued their search in the Land of the Dead. Here, they witnessed a glorious miracle. The mounds of the cemetery suddenly became a beautiful garden, abloom with exquisite roses, and they discovered, "There are no dead."

54

Life goes on always. Nothing perishes, there are only changes.

Finally they came to the end of their journey, weary and disappointed, for they had not found the Bluebird. They were particularly sad to bid farewell to their beautiful guide, Light. As she left, however, she consoled them by saying, "I shall not be far away—just over there in the land of the Silence of Things. Never forget that I am speaking to you in every spreading moonbeam, in every twinkling star, in every dawn that rises, in every lamp that is lit, and in every good and bright thought in your soul."

Back home again in their own little cottage, they wakened from their slumbers and tried to tell their unbelieving parents about some of the amazing adventures they had had. They were interrupted by a neighbour who came in on behalf of her sick daughter. The little girl knew she would get well if Tyltyl would only give her his dove. "Of course I will," Tyltyl exclaimed. As he reached for the cage, he cried in amazement, "Why, it's blue! It's the Bluebird that we were looking for. He was here at home all the time!"

The wonderful thing about the search for the Bluebird is that it was found as it was being given away. That is also the eternal secret of success in the quest for happiness; it can be found only as it is shared.

The Bluebird

If you would seek the Bluebird,
　　You need not journey far,
For it will come on flashing wings
　　To find you where you are.

If you should keep it in a cage,
　　Just for yourself alone,
The colours will turn grey and drab.
　　Some day it will have flown.

But if you give your bird away,
　　This "magic" you shall see;
Your bird will ever with you stay,
　　Blue as the skies 'twill be.

THE SHEPHERD'S SONG

ONE of the most beautiful poems ever written is the Shepherd's Song or Psalm. Though it is centuries old, its spiritual appeal is still strong in this twentieth century. The inspiration for the poem came to a young shepherd lad watching his sheep under the night skies. Experiencing the nearness and the overshadowing care of God, he thought of his own deep concern for his sheep on the hillside around him.

As a simple shepherd boy, guarding his father's sheep on the lonely hills, singing his songs through the long night watches, David passed through adventure after adventure. As the years went by, he experienced danger, suffering, and humiliation, but he knew also triumph, fame, and the highest honour his country could offer. In what was the Golden Age of Israel, he ruled in Eastern splendour. No other poet in history rose from the vocation of shepherd boy to that of king.

Shepherd life in the mountain regions of Asia has changed little from what it was more than two thousand years ago. In north India, I have seen the shepherds leading their flocks up over the mountains in the early spring, into the cooler and more fertile valleys beyond the foot-hills of the Himalayas. The shepherd still lives with and for his sheep. Going ahead of them, the shepherd picks out the easiest and safest way for the sheep to follow. He wears a loose garment, woven of wool, and about his waist a long rope serves as a belt. In the folds of the gar-ment, he often carries the helpless little lambs, and he uses the rope to rescue sheep which have slipped over a preci-pice. He finds the green pastures where there is nourish-ment and rest for them. In the mountainous country, dangerous torrents rush down the ravines in winter and spring, and when summer comes the land is parched and thirsty, but the shepherd knows where quiet pools, cool and pure, are to be found. There he leads them "beside the still waters".

Sometimes a sheep wanders into vineyards or gardens. If it is caught, its life is forfeited to the owner of the land. The shepherd "restores" or redeems it, and leads it again in the right path, proud of his own good name. Never-theless, it is often necessary to pass through dangerous places where wild beasts lurk ready to spring. Through "the valley of the shadow of death", the shepherd leads the way, using his rod as a weapon to protect them and his staff to guide and comfort them.

He finds a level place with soft green grass, a "table" such as we might choose for an out-door meal. Even there the sheep may be "in the presence of their enemies", for vipers are known to come out of holes in the ground, and sometimes it is necessary to build small fires for protection.

At the close of day, the shepherd stands at the opening to the fold and, as the sheep pass one by one, he inspects them. He has a horn filled with oil to anoint a bruised or bleeding part, and for the thirsty or weary sheep he has "a cup running over". The shepherd continues his watch over them, long after the sheep have been placed in the fold and the stars have come out. The trusting sheep know that no harm can come near them. "For surely goodness and mercy will follow" them always, as they remain safely in the care of the good shepherd.

What does it mean for us today to say or sing this old familiar song, "The Lord is my Shepherd"? Amid all the complexities and problems of modern life, it is a comforting realization to know that the Good Shepherd is still guiding and protecting us. To know that One, all-wise and all-loving, goes ahead and sees the path more clearly than we can ever see it, gives us assurance and courage. Whether we are weak or wilful, whether we wander or get completely lost, we cannot get beyond the reach of the Shepherd's untiring, searching love.

> I know not where His islands lift
> Their fronded palms in air;
> I only know I cannot drift
> Beyond His love and care.[1]

[1] John Greenleaf Whittier, "The Eternal Goodness".

Jesus, in His story of "The Lost Sheep", brought out the same truth. No sheep could get so hopelessly lost that the shepherd could not find it. Even though his ninety-nine sheep were safe and sheltered, the shepherd continued his search until the wandering one also was safe in the fold.

We, too, like sheep, are often stubborn, going our own unpredictable way, stupid, following the whims of others, dumb, making the same mistakes over and over again. But the Good Shepherd persistently brings us back into the right paths where we are conscious of His love and care.

Life's Trail

When in the silent woods you sometimes wander
    Following a winding trail without a fear,
Perhaps you've known a momentary panic,—
    The path you followed seemed to disappear.

The tangled green of branches closed about you,
    The sunlight dimmed, the shadows closely pressed.
Suddenly you're lost, and greatly frightened.
    Is there no sign, to show which way is best?

Out on the trail of Life you go light-hearted,
    For many are the joys encountered there;
Here too you find ofttimes your path obstructed,
    And wonder how you can proceed, and where.

If only in those deep perplexing moments
    We could be certain that whate'er betide,
Through doubtings and through fears the way will open,
    And God be ever with us as a Guide.

A FLIGHT OF BIRDS

EARLY in October, I climbed one evening to Dakona-wida Lookout, the highest point in camp, where one can look over a wide expanse of forest and lake. The autumn colours were still gorgeous and the sunset was beautiful. Suddenly there appeared from the north a faint, black, V-shaped design of birds, winging their way southward. I watched intently as they flew overhead. It was possible to identify them as a flock of wild geese, probably Canada geese, who had been summering in the tundras of the Arctic, and were now on their way to a southern clime.

Later, in the middle of the night, there came an ominous crash of thunder, the sky was streaked with chain lightning, and the rain poured down in torrents. While the storm raged, I remembered the V-shaped formation of birds winging south. Never before had the wonder of the migration of birds struck me as forcibly. While the wind pounded the waves against the rocks, and the lightning revealed the wild swaying of the trees, I thought of those frail wings beating their way against the storm, of goslings and ganders holding together in close formation. How amazing is the migratory flight of the birds!

I listed in my mind the essentials for a camper on a camping trip; I thought of compass, flashlight, packsacks, food, matches, raincoat and blankets. These southward-bound campers, the wild geese, travelled light. They had no compass to guide them through the night skies and keep them true to their course; no flashlight to il-lumine the darkness, only the frequent streaks of light-ning; no food for even a snack *en route*. Nevertheless, they had resources within themselves to make the long, wearisome journey. The ceaseless rhythmic beat of their powerfully-built wings would carry them through the trackless skies. Their mysterious intuition would take them to their far-off destination.

Some months later I travelled by plane to Florida. We motored one morning to a State Park to visit the lovely lagoons where many water birds were known to congre-gate. As we watched the tall blue herons and white egrets standing statuesque among the rushes, suddenly, from a clump of reeds at the edge of the water, rose a flock of wild geese. "Why those are Canada geese!" I exclaimed in astonishment. My thoughts went back immediately to an autumn hilltop, thousands of miles northward, where I had glimpsed them, probably midway in their long journey.

The distances the birds travel on their long migrations

are unbelievable. The curlews, for instance, are known to spend their summers in the tundras of the far north and their winters in Argentina. Six thousand miles they fly to the haunts of their own choosing. The tiny, brilliant-hued humming birds that hover above our blue delphiniums during the camp days seek the blossoms of far-off Mexico when the season ends. How fast they fly! Experts declare that certain birds can fly three miles a minute, even against wind and storm. There are tides of feathered life moving north and south with a regularity and a certainty through the ages, reminding us of the unfailing tides of the ocean and the trade winds. The mystery of these migratory flights turns our thoughts to the Creator. Before He made man, He fashioned the birds, and added to their other endowments of intuition and flight, the gifts of exquisite plumage and incomparable song.

> O the depths of the riches
> Both of the wisdom
> And knowledge of God.
> How unsearchable are His judgements
> And His ways past finding out.[1]

> There is a Power whose care
> Teaches thy way along the pathless coast—
> The desert and illimitable air—
> Lone wandering, but not lost.

[1] Romans xi, 33.

64

He who, from zone to zone,
Guides through the boundless sky thy certain flight,
In the long way I must tread alone
Will lead my steps aright.[1]

---

[1] William Cullen Bryant, "To a Waterfowl".

Miracles

A camper once was heard to say,
"There are no miracles today.
No miracles today at least
Like Scripture tales from out the East."

"So young, so sure," God seems to sigh.
"How small your world. How low your sky.
So deaf, so blind," He seems to say,
"To wonders of the every day."

No miracles? Awake from sleep!
Arouse your mind from slumber deep.
Each phase of life, could we but see,
Is all imbued with mystery.

The sun and stars still swing through space,
Held within their destined place.
Eternal law the tides obey
On far-off shores by night and day.

Birds wing their flight when summer's past
To distant lands o'er oceans vast.
Each feathered throat repeats its song
Familiar, true, through centuries long.

The Springtime comes through snow and hail
Bringing violets without fail.
New dreams still stir dull hearts awake
Revealing upward trails to take.

Great Spirit of Infinity,
Have patience till we learn to see
Thyself revealed each passing hour,
In the mystery of growth and power.

THE UPWARD REACH

HAVE you ever stood on the shore across from Niagara Falls and watched the mighty volume of green and white water tumbling over the precipice? Have you listened to the thunderous roar and been fascinated by the great clouds of mist and foam and rainbow-coloured spray rising from the depths below? Have you ever imagined you were an early explorer, coming suddenly upon this breath-taking spectacle for the first time? At that time the shores were bordered with great pine forests. How startled and sceptical you would have been if a prophetic voice had whispered in your ear, "Some day these forests will be gone, and great power plants will line these shores. Tremendous dynamos, generating electricity, will send the power of Niagara hundreds of miles across the land, to light cities and towns, to run subways and streetcars, and to turn the wheels in thousands of factories."

How like a fantasy of the imagination it would have seemed! Yet in a few short years this amazing dream has become a reality. We push a button when we enter a dark room and the power of Niagara floods the whole

68

place with light. We pick up a telephone receiver and electric energy enables us to hear the sound of a voice from the other side of the world. We turn a dial and watch and listen to happenings and dramas as they take place thousands of miles away. Even to us it is almost unbelievable. To our great-grandparents it would indeed have seemed supernatural. We, in our age of countless inventions, accept, as commonplace, things that are no less miraculous because they are daily occurrences.

There is, however, an even greater mystery in the universe than that of electricity. An undreamed-of force for transmitting light and spiritual energy is available in the sphere of the inner life. This mysterious force is our contact with God through prayer. In the simplest terms, prayer is a communication line between God and ourselves.

> Chief of all Thy wondrous work
> Supreme of all Thy plan,
> Thou hast put an upward reach
> Within the heart of Man.

We cannot understand it, and we may be as unaware of it as our ancestors were of electricity, but prayer is, and has been through the centuries, the greatest unrealized source of power in the world. We can understand the link of friendship between individuals, but how difficult we find it to conceive and make use of a line of spiritual communication between ourselves and the unseen Creator.

If radio's slim fingers
Can pluck a melody from night
And toss it o'er a continent or sea;
If the soft-petaled notes of a violin
Are blown o'er mountains, or a city's din;
If songs like fragrant roses
Are culled from thin blue air,
Then how can mortals wonder
If God hears prayer?

Mortals have always wondered! But as certainly, through the ages, they have inevitably lifted their hearts to God in their times of need, fear and danger,—perhaps more infrequently in their times of joy, thanksgiving and praise. Prayer is turning to God, our Father, as naturally as a flower turns to the sun. The essential thing in prayer is that it be sincere, not necessarily long, nor eloquent, nor spoken, but that it be a true expression from the inmost heart reaching out to the Eternal Father.

The unlimited power of prayer has been available since "man became a living soul", but like unharnessed Niagara, this Divine power has not been fully realized nor utilized. Great souls in all ages, however, have drawn on the resources of prayer and have proved its power in their lives.

More things are wrought by prayer
Than this world dreams of.

Abraham Lincoln said, "I have often gone to my knees in

the certain conviction that I had nowhere else to go."
Martin Luther said, "The more I have to do, the greater
is my need to take time to pray." We turn to God in our
weakness, to be made strong, in our bewilderment to be
given wisdom, and in our sense of sin to be forgiven.
"We kneel how weak, we rise how full of power." For
all our varied needs, we are given new resources.

Resources

Be thankful for the task too great for you,
    The plan that seems too large for you alone,
The need demanding better than your best
    Which draws you humbly to the Father's throne.

For there the finite meets the Infinite,
    And human limitations melt away:
God's great reserve of kindling, conquering power
    Is ours to draw from for the hardest day.

THE MIRACLE—YOU

WHAT a strange, dull world it would be if we did not possess the gift of choice! Like clocks wound up, or some mechanical toy, we would move automatically; or, like winds and waves, we would be driven by undeviating forces over which we had no control. Instead, we are free creatures with wills of our own, possessing amazing powers to make decisions good or bad. What a staggering fact it is to realize! God, in a sense, has limited His own power over our lives by endowing us with free will. We can choose to do, or not to do.

Each of us is a creation of God and we inherit His Divine gift, the will to choose, to reason, to dream, to create and to pray. He has, however, placed upon us responsibility for the use of His gift. We have a particular part to play in life.

All the world's a stage,
And all the men and women merely players.

After long centuries we take our places on the stage of history for a short space of time. Each of us has a unique and original role to play for which there is no understudy.

73

It is a thrilling thought to realize that never before has there been a *you* in all the centuries that have gone and never will there be another *you* in all the centuries that are to come. No other person can make the special contribution it is in your power to make, in your home, in your school, in your profession. It is essential, therefore, that you appraise yourself and place a high and sacred value on your own distinctive personality, the you that is *you*.

A story is told of a great concert conductor who, in the middle of an important rehearsal, stopped the music because he missed the special notes of a young musician in the back row. It was the bell-ringer's part to sound three notes, but his instrument seemed to him insignificant compared to the violins, cellos, and flutes. Thinking thus, he failed to strike his bells. "I miss the three notes of the bell-ringer," said the conductor. "When those particular notes are not sounded there is something lacking in the perfect harmony of the music." So, too, if we fail to play our special part there is something missing in the symphony of life.

Jesus, more than anyone who ever lived, knew and appreciated the value of the individual. He said, "What does it profit a man (or a boy, or a girl) if he gain the whole world and lose his own soul." Nothing we can ever gain—wealth, power, popularity or fame—can take the place of our God-given potential personality. The tragedy is that our own soul may be lost by copying others, instead of being guided by God to make our own choices and decisions. He who created us, with our special gifts and distinctive personalities, knows our *best*, and He alone can help us to achieve that ideal.

Life is made up of choices, not always between good and bad, but usually between good and best. Robert Louis Stevenson says: "We are damned, not for being bad, but for being satisfied to be only tolerably good."

> God has His best things for the few
> Who dare to stand the test.
> He has His second-best for those
> Who will not have His best.

The unfolding of personality is a miracle in itself, but more amazing still is the fact that by our own choices and decisions, we may each play, with God's guidance, a unique role in the Divine plan.

> All I could never be
> All men ignored in me,—
> This I was worth to God whose wheel the pitcher shaped.[1]

[1] Robert Browning, "Rabbi Ben Ezra".

You

Is it not a marvellous thing
    That all the long years through,
Since the world's beginning
    There never was a *You*.

All down the avenue of Time
    As dawn the centuries new,
The Future will not reproduce
    A duplicate of *You*.

The greatest role, to be *Yourself*,
    Enacting on life's stage
The script that's copyrighted
    For a special personage.

It is truly awe-inspiring
    When this sacred fact you view;
Your world holds naught more precious
    Than the *You* that is in *You*.

The same holds true of every soul
    Within his separate sphere;
The glorious chance to play his part
    Is always *Now* and *Here*.

A DAY OF ONE'S OWN

"PIPPA PASSES", a poem by Robert Browning, is the story of a little girl in an Italian hill town. Pippa worked in a silk factory and had only one holiday in the year. Sunday was God's day. All through the year Pippa looked forward to the day which she called, "my own day". Every hour belonged to her, to plan as she wished.

Stepping out into the morning sunshine on her own glad day, Pippa sang her happy little song:

> The year's at the spring,
> And day's at the morn;
> Morning's at seven;
> The hillside's dew-pearled,
> The lark's on the wing;
> The snail's on the thorn;
> God's in His heaven
> All's right with the world.

How Pippa spent her joyous day in the out-of-doors and the unconscious influence of her song on the lives of many people is a fascinating and inspiring story.

How wonderful it would be if each of us could have a special red-letter day to be called "a day of one's own",

77

or a Pippa Day. A camper would most certainly want to spend the day in the out-of-doors. How eagerly you would plan for your day and, when dawn came, you might set forth singing your own little song:

This is the day I call my own.
Out and away I'll fare alone.
Everywhere some fresh surprise
Will greet my grateful wondering eyes.
I'm glad for a sky of azure blue
And meadows sparkling with gems of dew.
I'm glad for a path 'mong birches white
And a book, and a lunch for an appetite.
The whole day's mine, go where I will,
Along the shore, or up the hill.
Beside a stream I'll rest, and say,
"Thank you God for a lovely day!"

A day is a wonderful thing and we only get one day at a time. No one can ever buy or beg an extra day, nor can it ever be lived over again. It is like a sheet of white paper on which we write with indelible ink something which can never be erased. Each day becomes part of us, for Time is the immortal stuff of which our lives are woven. A day of one's own is an extra special day, one to keep in our Book of Memory.

Free time may be of immeasurable value in our lives. For most of us, our days are mapped out. We follow schedules through school and college days. Later years bring an increasing number of engagements, appointments, and perhaps routine jobs. A hike through fragrant forests with a sense of awareness, a paddle by the shore with open eyes for the still beauty of reflections, a rest under pine trees with time to gaze at the sky and dream— these are "re-creations", beneficial for body and soul.

> No one can fathom the depths of his nature
> Who has not checkered his life with solitude.[1]

Suppose you were an artist and painted a beautiful picture, would you not be disappointed if those who passed by never paused to look at it? God is continually painting vast canvases, with roseate dawns and flaming sunsets, with changing clouds and blue-wrapped hills, and, close at our finger tips, flowers and ferns hidden in the grasses. He knows that our souls need to feast on beauty in order to grow, otherwise He would not have been so lavish with light and colour, fragrance and song. We are the losers when we fail to pause, to admire and wonder.

> Out of your cage,
> Come out of your cage
> And take your soul
> On a pilgrimage.

When Good Fortune comes and gives to you a day of your own, plan for it, cherish it, as a most precious gift. Whether you climb a hill, or follow a trail, or explore a

[1] Thomas DeQuincey

shore line, you will find beauty everywhere, and refresh-
ment for your soul in its hours of freedom and relaxation.
When at last your happy day is over and you must turn
your footsteps homeward, pause before you lift the latch
and whisper a heart-felt thanks, for you have been a guest
of God in His out-of-doors.

A Holiday

I gave myself a holiday
  Under the open sky,
Knowing the need for a tall straight tree,
  To lift my dreams on high,
And the quiet strength of granite
  To match my standards by.

Turning off from the beaten paths,
  Leaving care behind,
The only pack for the winding trail,
  A free and open mind.
Off on a quest for beauty!
  Who knows what one shall find?

It was good to go adventuring
  That lovely summer day,
For in the open spaces
  I tossed my doubts away:
Then felt a Presence immanent
  And knew I needs must pray.

FLOUR AND SALT

UNTIL recently, an old lady lived on the main street of our little village and it was one of my frequent pleasures to call on her. One had only to mention the phrase, "the old days", to bring a wistful look into her brown eyes and send her back along a trail of memory to pioneer days. She loved to talk about "the old days" and I always listened, spell-bound, to her tales of adventure. She described in detail the long trek into the backwoods district when, at the age of sixteen, she and her mother and small sister hiked over fifty miles from "the end of steel". The trail had been blazed in the spring by her father and two brothers. They had made a tiny clearing in the dense pine forest and had erected a one-room log cabin. Then the men-folks had gone out in August to escort the mother and daughters to their new home.

As they hiked through the wilderness each carried as heavy a load as he could manage. Among the necessities were a few clothes, home-spun blankets, some tools, a gun, and fishing tackle. The only food that it was essential to bring was flour and salt, for game and fish and

82

berries were plentiful *en route*. One luxury, however, was carried with great care and pride. It was a small square of glass, for the cabin was to possess one small window.

As the old lady talked about their adventures and hardships, the tale that always touched me most deeply was the story of their first Christmas. Two days before Christmas it was necessary for the father and brothers to make a trip to a settlement fifteen miles distant, to purchase the two essentials, flour and salt. They expected to return the afternoon before Christmas, but a terrific blizzard blew up and the snow piled high against the tiny cabin. By afternoon the trail was completely obliterated, but still the mother and daughters watched hopefully through the window. Then darkness came suddenly and the storm increased in fury. Branches crashed from the giant pine trees and the little pane of glass was completely covered with snow and ice. In the midst of the storm it was necessary for sixteen-year-old Mary to go out and replenish the dwindling supply of firewood. In the blackness of the night she heard the frightening howl of wolves. "But I never let that fire go out!" boasted the old lady, each time she retold the tale. "Though never before had I sawed a log right through by myself, I did it that Christmas Eve. All night long I tended the fire, for mother was expecting a baby."

Christmas morning dawned bright and clear, and

83

the drifted snow sparkled with diamonds. About noon, to their joy and relief, they suddenly heard a shout and the two girls bundled up in their coats and ran toward the opening in the woods to greet the returning weary travellers, and to lighten their loads. "Oh, we were so happy,—so *very* happy!" said the story-teller. "I shall never forget that first Christmas!"

Once, as the story-teller finished, I made the mistake of saying "I suppose there were no Christmas presents that year!" How stupid it was to make that remark! Her brown eyes blazed and she spoke rebukingly. "Christmas presents! We were thankful for flour and salt!"

Next Christmas morning when you are surrounded by tissue paper, stickers, ribbons, cards, and a lavish supply of gifts, I wish it were possible for me to place on top of your pile of presents a little book, suitably illustrated, entitled, "The Story of Mary Duke's Christmas". However, you can unwrap this little book in memory and picture a tiny log cabin with one small window, and a family that was thankful for flour and salt.

Perhaps we have travelled too far and too fast from those pioneer days of our grandparents or great-grandparents. Life has become easy and comfortable and we take so many good things for granted. We forget those who blazed our trails in this young land, whose endurance and hardships and courage laid the foundations for our

84

luxurious living, and our country's spectacular development.

There used to be an old hymn which was a favourite among the pioneers of a by-gone day:

> Count your many blessings
> Name them one by one,
> Then it will surprise you
> What the Lord has done.

How can we count the gifts and opportunities that we enjoy today? Ours is one of the favoured countries of the world, and we are blessed with a security, freedom, and prosperity unsurpassed anywhere. "To whom much is given, of him much is required." What a debt we owe!

> Service is the rent we pay
> For our room on earth.

Proportionately high is the debt we owe in service.

The Pioneer

Only a tiny pane of glass
    Set into logs, rough-hewn,
Beyond—the interminable forest,
    And the call of the wolf and the loon:
But theirs was a brave new land to make,
Of the trackless wild and the lonely lake.

Few were the humble comforts known,
    Yet, proudly and gladly, they
Created with skilful fingers
    The essentials of every day,
Jellies and soap, candles and clothes,
And the little gardens, set in rows.

Early the dark comes creeping down,
    The pines are etched on the sky,
There's a candle lit in a cabin,
    And the sound of a lullaby.
Oh, fold your hands, and rest at last,
Brave pioneer of our country's past!

Ours is a picture window,
    And oh, so wide the view!
So smooth for us the highways,
    The luxuries, so new!
But a clarion call rings strong and clear,
"Our land still needs the pioneer!"

THE WORLD IS ROUND

I WAS starting off on a trip around the world. Friends and relatives had gathered at the station to see me off, and among them was a six-year-old neighbour. She took me aside and stated positively and warningly, "I don't believe the world is round. If it is, you'll fall off the other side." "Watch for a post card," I said, "and promise to be at the station when I return. You will see me leaving in a few minutes on a train going toward Vancouver and the Pacific Ocean. If I come back by way of the Atlantic Ocean and Montreal, you will know the world is round, won't you?" She nodded her head, but continued to look sceptical.

Eleven months later I stepped off the train at the same station and the small friend was waiting for me. After some of the excitement of greetings had subsided, she slipped up beside me with her eyes shining. Her only remark was, "You did, didn't you! It is, isn't it!"

Yes, it truly is! The world is round and it is all *one* world. There is no favoured "top-side" on which the sun shines more brightly, and there is no "underneath side". The mighty globe on which we live swings through space, and the sun gives to all lands, alternate periods of light and darkness.

> The sun that bids us rest is waking
> Our brethren 'neath the western sky.

One encounters many different races, listens to a confusing variety of languages, and sees a great number of different customs and costumes as one travels on a world tour. It is evident, however, that in spite of all our differences, we have many things in common. The first unmistakable realization of this came to me at Yokohama when I saw a returning Japanese man affectionately greeted at the dock by a young woman with tears in her eyes, and a small kimono-clad child, dancing with happy excitement. Laughter and tears are the same in all lands. Suffering and need, love and gratitude, courage and sacrifice exist everywhere, irrespective of race, colour, or creed.

Stepping off the ship in the beautiful harbour of Hong Kong, I was warmly greeted by a Canadian friend who said, "I am so glad you arrived today! You are just in time to pin the wings on the angels." Of course, this sounded absolutely foolish and I stared at her in complete bewilderment until she explained, "Tonight we are having our Nativity Play at the Chinese Y.W.C.A., and you could be of great assistance back stage." So it happened that my first introduction to Chinese girls was when I "pinned the wings on the angels". I learned a very important lesson that night among those happy, excited teen-agers. I learned that the differences between the races are superficial compared to the fundamental things we have in common.

> I used to think that foreign girls
>   Lived far across the sea,
> Until there came a letter
>   From a Chinese girl to me:
> "Dear Foreign Friend," the note began
>   As plain as plain could be.
> I'm wondering now who's *foreign*,
>   That other girl,—or me.

Many young women from the Orient and Europe have been guests in our Canadian camps. They have contributed much to our happiness by sharing with us a knowledge of their crafts, and information about their own lands. They soon became good friends, and through them a link was established with the country to which they were returning. These happy relationships are like bridges of friendship.

Many of you have travelled over the Peace Bridge between Canada and the United States. That bridge commenced with two slender cables stretched across the wide expanse of the Niagara River. Afterwards foundations were built deep and strong on both sides, and the opposite shores were eventually linked together with a massive bridge. The bridge commemorated an inter-

89

national friendship and a hundred years of peace.

Our international friendships are only slender cables, but if we strive to keep them strong and true, they will help in building the bridges,—bridges of understanding and fellowship, which in our day are sorely needed between nations.

> Underneath the seas all islands are one.
> Underneath the creeds, all humanities are one.

One World

Vast are the deserts of the world,
    Wide-stretched the lonely sea,
High the forbidding mountains
    Standing guard eternally;
But matchless are the countries
    North, south, and east and west,
Which our brothers call "The Homeland",
    And which each considers *best*.

Though we contemplate each other
    As an alien, and quite odd,
We're all of us related
    In the family of God.
We have never lived as neighbours;
    Hate has kept us wide apart,
Yet we have a bond in common,
    An understanding heart.

Our language may be different
    And the costumes that we wear,
But we know the balm of laughter,
    And pain and sorrow share.
The Golden Age will surely come
    When fearful warfare ends,
When we esteem our fellow men,
    And greet them as our friends.

If we would be the builders
 Of the bridges yet to be,
'Cross the racial gulfs and canyons
 That frustrate sodality;
We must strive to make the cables
 Strong and steadfast till they seem
The causeway Peace has visioned,
 Making true her age-long dream.

GOD'S WHISPER

THE hydrogen bomb was recently referred to in an editorial as "The Fact", a sure and certain reality of which we, today, must be seriously aware. "For the first time in history an instrument exists by which man could wipe out the civilization of his fellowmen on this planet. Whether one lives in New York or Moscow, London or Toronto, Paris or Rome, no one is out of range of the bomb's destructive power."

You who are young and carefree probably never allow the dread shadow of the bomb to cross your minds or weigh your spirits down. Your days, especially in holiday time, are full of joy and adventure. Because you are young, however, and yours is the world of tomorrow, you will grow up in a world very different from ours of yester-year. The existence of an instrument with such dire possibilities causes reasonable fear and dark foreboding in all parts of the world. The only hope discernible is that nations with power to use the bomb may be trusted not to use it.

Another force exists in the world, however, which could also be referred to as "The Fact", a sure and certain reality. That Fact is God, our loving Father. "His faith-fulness endureth forever." This is an anchor to hold us steady and give us confidence and strength. Evidence of God's faithfulness is clearly and continually before our eyes.

Every year without fail, we watch the seasons come in regular succession.

> Never yet was a springtime
>   Late though lingered the snow,
> That the sap stirred not at the whisper
>   Of the south wind sweet and low;
> Never yet was a springtime
>   When the buds forgot to blow.[1]

Every night, unless clouds intervene, the stars can be seen in their destined places. By the stars, mariners have steered their ships for countless ages. By the stars, Green-wich time is given to us, "the clock that is always right". Every morning a new day is given to us and night brings her gifts of darkness and sleep. These are some of the dependable things revealing to us that Divine faithfulness "which endureth forever".

In a world teeming with millions of people, we ask the question: "Does the God of the seasons, the stars, the days and the nights, have any special concern for us as individuals?" Stop and think! The fact that we *can* think, and *are* individuals is the amazing answer. God is

[1] Margaret Elizabeth Sangster, "Awakening".

94

concerned with each and every member of His great family.

He speaks to us through an inner voice. God's whisper can spur ordinary human beings to accomplish extraordinary results. It was God's whisper which caused Joan of Arc, the Maid of France, to rally an army to save her beloved country. It was God's whisper that sent Florence Nightingale from a comfortable home in London to face the dirt, and misery, and inefficiency of a soldiers' hospital in the Crimea. "The lady with the lamp" blazed a trail for the many thousands of nurses who have followed her shining example. It was God's whisper that sent Albert Schweitzer, the world-famous organist, theologian, and surgeon into the depths of French Equatorial Africa to live a life of service among the natives.

God's whisper in the hearts of men everywhere would be a saving force of love, more powerful than the dreaded hydrogen bomb. It would be a Divine insurance against this devastating force being used by man against mankind. It would ensure that the amazing possibilities of the bomb would be used instead for the good of the world.

You, who are young, have a grave responsibility awaiting you in the world of tomorrow. You must help to make come true the age-long dream of "peace on earth, good will toward men". In the fact of God's love and the faithfulness "which endureth forever", lies our confidence and hope. Nevertheless, God uses men as instruments to work out His purposes, and God's whisper will give the challenge and the guidance needed by each one of us for the coming atomic age.

The Voice

Faint as the flutter of pinions
    Gentle as brooding bird,
Soft as the breath of an evening breeze,
    Or the murmur of waves half-heard;
Patient, impassioned, persistent,
    There falls on the inner ear
The still small voice of the Infinite
    Calling the soul to hear.

What is the quiet message
    The Voice would give to me?
Is it a whispered summons
    To an undreamed destiny?
Will it mean a clearer vision,
    To glimpse a plan unroll,
Where a humble, earnest effort
    Is part of a vaster whole?

The heart made wise by silence,
    Alert with the listening ear,
Will be attuned to interpret
    The voice of the Presence near.
Life will take on new meaning,
    Clearer will stretch the road,
For doubt and fear are banished
    By the still small voice of God.

THE BELL OF KIYOMIZU

SITTING around a wood-fire in a Tokyo home, where we had been supper guests, a group of young people were chatting together. As we represented several different countries, it was suggested that each of us tell a story of his own land. Interesting tales were told that night in the firelight, but the story which remained most clearly in my memory was told in very careful English by a Japanese university student. This was his story:

The Abbot of a certain temple in Kyoto was greatly distressed because the people were not coming to worship. Once the great temple, with its red-lacquered pillars, had been crowded but now it was attended by only a few worshippers. The Abbot called his priests together in council to discuss what steps should be taken to stimulate anew the interest and devotion of their people.

They decided to make a great temple bell. For this bell they would solicit, not just a few large gifts from rich people, but they would collect many small gifts over the whole countryside. Thus, the greater number having helped with the project, the interest would be more widespread and the success more certain.

The priests set forth with much enthusiasm to collect gifts, large and small, from rich and poor. That no one might feel his gift was too small and insignificant, they asked that the money be donated in copper coins, which later would be melted down to fashion the bell.

One young priest went through the streets of the city without any enthusiasm. He went from house to house, ringing his small bell and chanting his plea halfheartedly, but he met with no response. He became less interested than ever. At the close of the day he found himself chanting his petition outside a very poor little cottage beside an open gutter. An old woman stepped out of the doorway and handed him a one-rin piece. "It is all I have," she said. He looked contemptuously at the one-rin piece, which is the smallest of all coins, and with disgust he tossed it into the gutter, saying, "Art thou a fool to think that a temple bell can be made from a one-rin piece?" The old woman turned sorrowfully away and the young priest returned to the temple.

Money poured in from villages and cities and from farmers and fishermen. At last the Abbot announced, "We have now collected enough coins to mould a very fine bell, such as the country has never seen nor heard." The copper coins were melted down in a great furnace and poured into a mould. After several days it was cool and set.

A large company of people gathered to watch the

99

hanging of the bell. It was hung with great ceremony in the temple court, on two huge red-lacquered pillars, with a strong cross beam. The Abbot and the priests, clad in their official robes of red and purple brocade, stood nearby in the courtyard among the high cryptomeria trees and the stone lanterns. The large carved wooden beam was then suspended for striking the bell. All sounds were hushed as everyone waited expectantly to hear the deep musical tone of the bell.

Two priests swung the beam back and forth, then it struck the great bell, but the sound which came forth was hollow and harsh. Everyone looked at each other in dismay. The chief bellmaker was summoned to examine it. "There is a tiny crack in the inside of the bell," he said. "It is no bigger than a one-rin piece."

The disappointment was great. The bell was lowered again, and the Abbot ordered that it be melted down and recast. "Since the bell must be remade," he said, "it would be well to gather more coins to make it even larger. Let our temple and God be glorified by an exceedingly great bell."

Again coins poured into the hands of the priests and again the bell was recast and ready to be hung. The great assembly of people stood in the temple courtyard waiting. When the heavy beam swung back and hit the bell, once more it gave forth a harsh and hollow sound.

The old Abbot bowed his head and was silent. The priests shook their heads and said, "There is some evil spirit which prevents the bell from giving forth its true music." The chief bellmaker examined it. "I cannot account for it," he said, "but again there is a crack no bigger than a one-rin piece."

Then the young priest, who had been so ungrateful to the old woman, could no longer stand the torturing of his own conscience. He stepped out from among all the priests and remorsefully told what he had done. The Abbot said to him, "Until that one-rin piece is restored, the bell will not be perfect. Go forth and search until it is found." The young priest said, "It is now three years since the old woman gave it to me. I threw it into the gutter and it sank deep into the mud. Nevertheless, I will search until I find it." "Perchance," said the Abbot, "if we could get the forgiveness of the old woman and she were to give another coin, all would be well." So the Abbot and the priests in all their ceremonial robes of brocade went in procession to the poor home of the old woman. They removed their sandals and, standing in bare feet with bowed heads, they chanted prayers of penitence.

As they stood thus, they saw slowly rising from the mud of the gutter a lotus plant. While they watched, the great white lotus blossom, the most beautiful and most sacred flower of the East, slowly opened its waxen petals, and there in the golden heart of the flower was a shining one-rin piece.

Reverently they took the coin. The bell was remoulded. Once again a great assembly gathered in the temple courtyard. The heavy beam was swung against the bell. The clear musical tone of it rang out over the hills and valleys, the city and the nearby villages. And because of its exceedingly deep-toned bell, the temple of Kiyomizu in Kyoto became one of the most famous in Japan.

That the value of small gifts is sometimes underestimated is the message of this story. You may think, "My gift to the world won't be worth two cents. I haven't outstanding gifts, nor any one special talent. I can never do as well as some people who are endowed with many gifts. Why, therefore, should I try?" When you are tempted to minimize your own importance, remember that the smallest coin was needed to make the perfect bell and the perfect music. Your gift may be small, but it may be the one note needed in the great symphony of life.

A Small Gift

It was a small gift:
Only five loaves and two fishes.
"Bring them to me," saith the Master.
When they were brought
He blessed them,
And a great multitude were fed.

Yours is a small gift,
Not worth much to the world?
"Bring it to me," saith the Master.
When it is offered up
And blessed by Him
Who knows what it then may become?

No gift is too small!
With His benediction upon it
An alchemy makes it Divine.
Given away, it glows.
Transmuted with vision and work,
It becomes a gift beyond dreams.

SAINT FRANCIS

IF there were a patron saint of campers, no doubt it would be Saint Francis. Seven centuries ago he sang his praises to God for sun and wind, fire and water, and all the beautiful things of the out-of-doors. Without doubt he would have given a joyous benediction to any sincere expression of reverence and worship, whether in an out-door camp chapel, roofed with sky, or in the solitary silences of the forest. The message he preached is like the song of birds and the music of winds. Where other saints overawe us with their holiness, Saint Francis captivates us with a sweet persuasiveness, an exuberant happiness, and an overflowing love for all creatures, great and small.

Though long years have passed since Francis was a lad, one can still visit his Italian village and live in memory the story of his life. Assisi, high in the hills, looks down over a wide plain. The roadway is so steep, as it winds upward among the silver olive trees, that even the big white oxen must strain hard to pull their carts up to the gates of the town. Within the walled village the streets are narrow and the houses have wide overhanging eaves.

In the year 1182, Saint Francis was born in Assisi and given the baptismal name of Giovanni Bernadoni. From the first, however, he was called by the nickname of Francesco. His father, a prosperous merchant, had just returned from trading in France where he had made a great deal of money. Francis was the pride and joy of his father and mother, and a favourite with the whole village. A happy, daring boy, he became a leader in games and every kind of fun and adventure. Though he was never out of mischief, he was never cruel or unkind.

As he grew older, Francis was still the gayest of all the young men of Assisi. Once, in a jester's costume, he led them on a merry dance through the streets, scandalizing the staid and solemn folk. He wore the costliest clothes and his purse was open to his friends, for his father grudged him nothing. A sad day came, however, when Francis fell ill and for days it was feared he would die. Though he slowly grew better, he was never quite as gay again. The old life lost its appeal. There was something he felt he must do in the world—some special work waiting for him.

Walking one day along the winding road, dreaming his dreams, he was stopped suddenly by a poor beggar who asked Francis to help him, "for the love of God". Startled from his day-dreams, Francis recognized the man as an old soldier who had fought with courage for his country. Without stopping to think, he pulled off his scarlet velvet cloak and tenderly wrapped it around the shoulders of the shivering old man.

He never thought of reward, but that night he had a dream or vision. Christ appeared to him and, leading him by the hand, showed him a great palace full of shining weapons and flags of victory. Each one was marked with a cross. As Francis gazed, he heard a voice saying, "I need faithful soldiers to fight under my banner."

With great joy Francis set forth next day to join the army but, in the quiet of the night, he again heard the voice of Christ telling him it was a different kind of service he required of His soldiers. Troubled and sad, Francis went back toward Assisi. As he walked through the ripening vineyards, he felt a sudden revulsion against all kinds of money-getting. While pondering these thoughts, he stopped outside the walls of the town by the chapel of San Damiano and knelt among the ruins. As he prayed, the Voice whispered, "Repair my church." Now Francis thought this meant he was to rebuild the walls. Glad to find real work to be done, he went joyfully home and took many precious things from his home to be sold in the market place. Returning to the little church, he offered the money to the old priest, telling him to rebuild the walls and make the chapel beautiful. The priest refused to accept the money, fearing that Francis

106

had done wrong and that his father would be angry.

His father was angry indeed. He did not mind Francis squandering money on clothes or pleasures, but he wanted no part in repairing an old church or spending for charity. He was furious with his son and locked him up in a cellar without food. That night his mother unlocked the door, listened to his story, and told him to flee. Again he took refuge in the ruined church with the old priest. In anger, his father brought the bishop to reprimand Francis. Gently the bishop reminded him that the money was not his to give. That, Francis realized, was true. There and then, with numerous old friends and citizens looking on, he took off his costly clothes. "Listen, all of you," he said, "until this time, I called this man my father. From now on, I will say only, 'My Father which is in heaven'."

Clothed in a rough brown tunic given to him by a poor labourer, Francis set forth, not as a monk aloof from the world, but as a troubadour, singing his glad songs of praise for petal and wing, tree and star.

> Give me the moon for a blanket,
> Give me the stars overhead;
> I'll make the hillside my door step,
> I'll make the meadow my bed.

"I am God's Jester," he would blithely say to the people. "Pay me by offering yourselves to Him." Gaily he did all the things he had previously disliked, nursing the sick,

107

even lepers, carrying burdens and begging for his simple meals. Then he came back to the little church outside Assisi, and with his own hands he began to rebuild the walls.

Disciples flocked to him unsought, first one of his rich young friends, then an eminent doctor of laws. The numbers soon grew to twelve. They called themselves "the poor brothers of Assisi" and their only rule was the one given by Christ to his apostles: "Go forth and preach; cure the sick and cleanse the leper. Freely you have received—freely give. Provide neither gold nor silver, nor script for your journey."

Throughout his life Francis had the same ready smile and happy nature. Though he knew poverty, hunger and cold, though he had no roof but the sky, though he went on long and dangerous journeys during the Crusades, he still kept his gaiety of spirit. He loved everything God had made. The animals and birds became his special friends. It was said that when he walked in the woods the birds perched on his shoulders and when he preached to them as "little sisters and brothers", he reminded them that they must never neglect to sing, "for song is praise to God".

A Song of Saint Francis

O Lord, we praise Thee for our Brother Sun,
Who brings us day, who brings us golden light;
He tells us of Thy beauty, Holy One.
We praise Thee too, when falls the quiet night
For Sister Moon, and every silver star
That Thou hast set in Heaven, clear and far.

For our brave Brother Wind, we give Thee praise;
For clouds and stormy skies, for gentle air;
And for our Sister Water, cool and fair,
Who does us service in sweet, humble ways;
But when the winter darkens, bitter cold,
We praise Thee every night and all day long
For our good friend, so merry and so bold
Dear Brother Fire, beautiful and strong;
For our good Mother Earth, we praise Thee Lord;
For the bright flowers she scatters everywhere
For all the fruit and grain her fields afford;
For her great beauty and her tireless care.

Saint Francis
(translated by Sarah Jewett)

A Saint

A little child one summer morn
    Within a chancel gazed
At a lovely stained-glass window,
    Through which the sunlight blazed.

Enshrined in glowing colours
    A gentle figure smiled
From out the lofty casement,
    Upon the wondering child.

"What is a saint?" she whispered,
    "It must be someone who
Is like a stained-glass window,
    And lets the light shine through."

CLIMBING THE MOUNTAIN

WEARING white buckskin, heavily beaded, and with an eagle feather in her headband, Dawendine presented a striking appearance. But more dramatic than her appearance was the spirited eloquence with which she told legends of her people, during the two summers she visited camp. Daughter of the Chief of the Mohawks, from the Six Nations' Reserve, Dawendine possessed an intense pride of race. Her wide knowledge embraced the colourful history, legends, and customs of the Mohawks. She was equally familiar with the stories of many tribes.

The light from the Council Ring fire lit up the tall silver birches, the eager faces of the wide circle of campers, and the slender figure of the Indian girl in white buckskin, as she told this legend of the Navajos.

Long ago the Chief of the Navajos wished to test the boys of the tribe, to find out whether they possessed fortitude, courage and leadership. The Navajo Indians lived then, as they still do, on the great plains near the foot of the towering Rocky Mountains.

The Chief called together the boys of the tribe and said, "Tomorrow at dawn you are to set forth. You are to climb the mountain which rises before you across the plains. I set no goal for you. I place no limits on the distance you may go, nor the time you may take. I only bid you climb. You may turn back wherever you wish. The only thing I ask of you is that you bring to me something from the spot where you turn back. Thus shall I know how high each of you has climbed."

The boys were keen for the adventure. Some of them were up before the dawn, eager to be away. The old Chief watched them all set forth. He stood gazing after them until they were out of sight across the plains. Hour after hour he waited and watched alone for their return.

In the early afternoon a group of boys came sauntering back together. In their hands they carried branches of the sage bush, which they handed rather hesitatingly to their Chief. "Why!" he exclaimed, with deep disappointment and rebuke, "You have not climbed at all. The sage bush grows at the far edge of the plains where the mountains only begin to rise. You have not climbed."

Later on, toward sunset hour, some more boys came back and they had in their hands branches of cottonwood. The Chief looked at them wistfully and said, "You boys only began to climb." A little later two boys returned bringing branches of cedar. "Ah," he said, "you climbed, but you only reached the spring, midway up the slope of

112

the mountain side. Why did you turn back so soon?"

Long after the stars had come out, two more boys came back. They were weary, and in their hands were branches of shrub pine. "You have done well," said the Chief. "You reached the steep high crags where only the shrub pine grows."

The old Navajo Chief was well aware that there was still one lad who had not returned. It was dark now and it was cold, but he waited, spending his solitary vigil out under the stars. As the first glow of early dawn came, he saw the last boy coming toward him. His face was radiant. His eyes were shining. "I have nothing in my hands, O Chief," he said. "Nothing grew at the heights to which I climbed. But oh, I saw something which none of the others have ever seen. I saw beyond the mountain-top to the shining sea."

The Chief said, "I knew it! I knew it! I saw it in the radiance of your face and in the light of your eyes. It matters not that you have nothing in your hands, for within you, you will keep forever a vision of the shining sea."

As we think of the story, "Climbing the Mountain", we realize it is a logical and inevitable fact that we get out of life, in proportion to what we put into it. We can keep to the plains and be satisfied with "sage bush" and the lesser rewards, or we can climb. Like the boys in the story, we are free to choose whether we shall continue to press on. The reward for persistence, endurance and courage may not be tangible, but in our hearts will be an inner satisfaction—perhaps a vision of "the shining sea", and a word of approbation.

One of the greatest joys of camp life is the opportunity to set forth on a camping trip. Whether your trip lies through familiar waters and well-worn trails or into the wilderness, there is an excitement about all the preparations. You spread out your map and eagerly trace the possible water-ways, trails, portages, camp sites and alternative routes.

It would be thrilling if we could spread out a map for the journey of Life, if we could see all the various routes for our choosing. But each of us travels alone into unexplored country. No ready-made map is at hand for your life or mine. The trail goes out into the unknown territory of the Future, into which no one has yet set foot. We can never guess nor prophesy the strange twists and turns our trail may take, but the glory and the wonder and, alas, the tragedy of it lie in the fact that our choices determine whether the trail shall be an upward-winding one.

> To every man there openeth
> A Way, and Ways, and a Way
> The High Soul climbs the High Way
> The Low Soul gropes the Low,

And in between, on the misty flats
The rest drift to and fro.
To every man there openeth
A High Way and a Low,
And every man decideth,
The Way his soul shall go.[1]

[1] John Oxenham, "The Ways".

Maps

Maps are such literal things,
    In essence, so matter of fact,
Mountains, lakes and curving roads,
    Apparent, and exact.

But maps have a subtle power:
    Spread one out on the floor,
Now, it's a "magic carpet",
    And you can go explore!

Fabulous lands you envision
    Travelling highways and streams,
Climbing hills and riding plains,
    Yours is a passport of dreams.

But Youth is ever eager
    One special map to discern,
The inscrutable map of the Future,
    Its puzzling routes to learn.

Yet neither saints nor seers
    Can Life's strange ways divine.
Each one must cipher for himself
    His own unique design.

Only the great Map-Maker
    Our way can apprehend.
Grant we may learn His chosen route,
    And keep it to the end.

MICHI KAWAI

MICHI KAWAI, in her book, *Sliding Doors,* wrote: "The doors of Japanese houses slide noiselessly along the grooves and have no keys and locks. My country wants no iron curtain." How eagerly we waited after the war was over for those sliding doors to open that we might have contact once again with dearly loved friends in Japan.

To a group of 'teen-age girls who long ago attended the first schoolgirls' camp of the Y.W.C.A. at Lake Couchiching, Michi Kawai was something out of a story book,—the very first Japanese girl that any of us had ever seen. We were fascinated with her beautiful flower-bordered crepe kimono and her gorgeous brocade obi with its flat bow at the back. In the camp setting of tents, pine trees, and rocky shores, the story-book guest from far-off Tokyo soon became one of us and we ceased to think of her as a foreigner.

While she chatted informally in the dining room, her artistic fingers created clever things from paper serviettes, birds, sail boats, fans and flowers. Meeting her in discussion groups, we realized her mind was quick and

117

challenging, and listening to her in formal addresses, we gained a new concept of world friendship from the vivid pictures of her own land.

One memorable day Michi and I walked along the rocky shore together. Reaching a point where a flat rock, jutting out into the lake, looked inviting, we sat down. Here we began talking about ourselves and the things that each of us wanted to do. Michi's father had been a Shinto priest of the Imperial Shrine at Ise. She remembered accompanying him, as a child, to the shrine when he went to worship in the evenings. "I can feel yet the awesomeness of the long walk under the dark cryptomeria trees, but when my father left me alone in the courtyard I was always terrified. The great trees looked like black giants and the wild monkeys chattered with their shrill cries. Later on when my father became a Christian, I was glad that I need never go there again."

After her father left the famous Ise Shrine, life became exceedingly difficult for her parents and the family became very poor. They moved to Hokkaido, an island in the far north of Japan. As a small child, she was sent to a mission school some distance from home in the northern city of Sapporo. Though very unhappy at first, and frightened of the foreign teacher with the fair hair, gradually "I learned to understand and love the American teacher". A wonderful opportunity came to Michi later because of the great interest she had taken in her studies. She was chosen as a scholarship student to go to the United States, and she spent four eventful years at Bryn Mawr College.

Opportunities of this kind came to few girls of the Orient. She told me what a deep sense of obligation had welled up within her, and what dreams had filled her imagination as she thought of what she would like to do when she returned to Japan. She was silent for a time, looking across the blue-green waters of Lake Couchiching, then she surprised me by saying, "I've come to the conclusion that Christianity does not make great demands upon you girls of America and Canada. You take it for granted. It does not cost you much. To a girl in Japan, being a Christian means beginning a new way of life. It means breaking with the past, and entering into a new and vital relationship with Christ." Then, to my sheer amazement, she said, "Will you pray with me for the girls of Canada?" What a shock! To pray, not for the girls of mission lands, but for the girls of Canada! Do you wonder that I have never forgotten Michi Kawai?

On two visits to Japan, I found my friend working out her dreams with unfailing vigour and enthusiasm. Under her leadership as National Secretary of the Y.W.C.A., work was begun for young women in the large cities of Tokyo, Yokohama, Kobe and Osaka. Countless numbers of girls in that rapidly-changing country found sympathetic help and fun at the attractive

Y.W.C.A. centres. I learned the secret of Michi's success while on a particularly delightful trip to Miyanoshita with her and Dr. Caroline MacDonald, our first Canadian secretary. On the train returning to Tokyo, Michi wrote these words in my diary:

> To the worker who can dream,
> And the dreamer who can work,
> Life surrenders all things.

When next I returned to Japan, one of her most precious dreams had become a reality. By dint of terrific work and tremendous faith, a girls' school of her own was already flourishing. Keisen Jogakuen (Fountain of Blessings) is now bringing new learning and a challenging outlook on life to thousands of girls in Japan. The thrilling story of this educational accomplishment is told in her book, *My Lantern*. The lighted lantern is the symbol of her school and a lighted lantern is a fitting symbol of her life.

For those of us who know the story of Michi Kawai, there is a challenge to keep our own little light trimmed and burning, that we may help chase away every trace of gloom and darkness in the world in which we live. Many of the deep shadows of international relationships might vanish if each of us would carry our own lighted lantern of faith and love.

A Tribute to Y.W.C.A. Pioneers

A debt is ours, to those of daring dreams
    Whose faith and vision reached beyond their day,
Blazing a trail for girlhood's eager feet,
    A trail that Time has made a broad highway.

A highway winding ever up and on,
    To friendship and adventure, joy and zest,
Leading towards "the more abundant life",
    And beckoning always on, to Life's high quest.

THE GOLDEN RULE

Do unto others as you would
that they should do unto you.

WHAT a concise and simple sermon! Twelve words
that sum up a relationship with others, which, if
universally practised, could change the world, and make
each life a source of blessing and happiness. Certainly it
is a pointed rebuke against unkindness, injustice and
cruelty. What was the occasion on which Jesus first used
those words? Perhaps it was a challenge flung at the
big bully of the village when Jesus was still a lad in Nazareth. Let us think about those boyhood years.

The main street of the small village was lined with
white-washed, flat-roofed houses, and little shops open to
the street. Probably the house of Joseph and Mary, with
the adjoining carpenter shop, was located here on the
busiest part of the main street. Though it was a quiet
village in itself, an historic road ran through it. Many
wayfaring folk travelled this highway, important officials
from far-off Rome on swift horses, tradesmen with heavily-
laden camels, peasants on donkeys or plodding along on
foot. All of them would pause *en route* at the village

well. Many of them, no doubt, stopped at the carpenter shop for repairs to carts, wheels or shafts.

Jesus, working with his father, Joseph, would have opportunities to meet a great variety of people,—Roman officers in shining brass helmets, swaggering with importance, wealthy merchants anxious about their precious caravans, and pilgrims from neighbouring villages eagerly travelling to the golden-domed temple at Jerusalem.

The neighbours and friends who lived in Nazareth all year round were the folk with whom Jesus would be well acquainted. There is no place like a little town in which to know one's neighbours, their faults and failings, their successes and tragedies, and their spontaneous helpfulness in any time of emergency. Those neighbours of Nazareth revealed to Jesus the heights and depths of human personality.

Jesus, so sensitive and loving Himself, must have been hurt deeply when He saw cruelty in any form, to animals, to helpless or handicapped people, and particularly to children. Not only hurts to the body, but deeper hurts which inflicted hidden wounds and sometimes brought tears, found a ready response from His sympathetic nature. It probably took great courage on His part when He first said, "Do unto others as you would that they should do unto you." To whom were those words first addressed? To older boys mistreating a child, to a mean neighbour exacting the last penny of a debt, to a bitter-tongued individual bringing tears to a sensitive soul? His sympathy was always with the one who was hurt.

These words, known everywhere as "The Golden Rule", were spoken by Jesus to a particular individual. But they are just as certainly a challenge to each one of us today, and mean little if we think of them only as an excellent rule for someone else. We must say deep in our own hearts, with all our strength of will and high resolve, "*My* golden rule shall be, to do unto others as I would that they should do unto me."

Often at the end of a camp season, as we look back over the happy days and joyous adventures, we realize that the only things that have marred our complete happiness have been the little unkindnesses. Camp life should, above all, teach us how to live happily with other people,— in other words, to live by the Golden Rule. It will take a lifetime of practice, but "Do unto others as you would that they should do unto you", is a rule of conduct which will bring entire and lasting satisfaction.

When You Are Kind

When you are kind, the sun shines down more brightly,
    And clouded skies reveal a fringe of light,
When all about is dark as blackest midnight
    Your candle gleam still pushes back the night.

When you are kind, the wayside smiles with flowers
    The atmosphere takes on a golden hue,
And even if the road turns steeply upward
    The climbing is less hard, because of you.

When you are kind, it is a wealth to treasure,
    A legacy of worth to hoard and hold;
For times of need, or hours of bitter sorrow
    Memory guards her coins of purest gold.

If it is in your power, this gift of kindness
    To someone struggling up life's trail to give,
Bestow on him, as you would wish to harvest,
    And you will know God's blessing while you live.

THE CAMP HYMN

SINCE "God, Who Touchest Earth with Beauty" appeared as a camp hymn, there have been many enquiries as to how and when it was written. These facts may be of interest to campers.

A prayer written in 1922 for our Council Ring ceremony gave first expression to the ideas which were later given poetical form.

> We thank Thee for the loveliness of Thy world. May we weave into the fabric of our character something of that beauty. Give to us the purity of springs and running water, the strength and steadfastness of rocks, the joy of dancing waves in sunlight, the straight uprightness of trees and the high uplift of Thy arching skies.

This was part of the Initiation Prayer, to be used only once each season. In the spring of 1925, however, an inspiration came to me, that the same ideas expressed in a hymn could be sung frequently. With surprising facility the poetic form took shape, and the verses were mailed to the late Magistrate James Edmund Jones of the Anglican Hymnal Committee, with a request that he suggest a suitable tune. Having been invited to his home, I listened as he sat at his pipe organ and played three tunes

126

from which a choice was to be made. When I chose the last one, he said, "That is the one I composed specially for the hymn, but I wanted to be certain that you liked it best. The tune will be called Glen Bernard."

The following year the American Camping Association offered a prize for a song or hymn. The Camp Hymn was awarded the prize and it was printed with music, in *Camping Magazine*, published in Chicago. Immediately, it became available to the camps of the U.S.A. When I attended a camp conference the following winter in Asheville, N.C., it was a surprise to learn that many camps were already using the hymn in their chapel services. At a camp in the Blue Ridge Mountains, the campers, themselves, had decided to sing the verses from cabin to cabin as a last good night after taps had sounded.

In Canada the hymn did not become known until some time later, when circumstances, which were most tragic, brought it into wider use. One Sunday evening the boys of a Church camp operating on Balsam Lake, paddled in a war canoe to a beautiful point to hold their vesper service. While the last flames of the sunset faded across the lake, the campers, having been given printed copies of the hymn, closed their service with the words, "God, who touchest earth with beauty". As they were paddling back to the camp, a sudden storm blew up. The war canoe capsized, and eleven of the twenty-six boys in the canoe were drowned. This was the greatest tragedy in the history of Canadian camping. Many were the acts of supreme heroism that dark night on a little northern lake. One little brother survived because his older brother "kept looking at me and telling me to hold on tight." A young leader deliberately swam off into the night, relinquishing his hold, that others, hanging on to the canoe, might have a better chance to survive. They proved themselves to be "strong and true".

At a memorial service in St. James Cathedral in Toronto, the camp hymn was sung, and when the newspapers reported the service, they printed both words and music. Shortly afterward the hymn was included in the song books of the Canadian Girls in Training and the Girl Guides of Canada, Great Britain, New Zealand and Australia. The Canadian Anglican hymn book and several American hymn books included it in new editions. Translations were sent to me in French, Spanish, Portuguese, Japanese, and the Cree Indian language. Several new tunes were composed, the best known being "Geneva", by C. Harold Lowden of Philadelphia, which is the tune most used in the United States.

An Indian school, the Shingwaulk School near Sault Ste. Marie, chose it as their school hymn. "Shingwaulk" in the Ojibway language means "pine tree", and the Indian boys and girls chose as their motto:

> Like the straightness of the pine tree,
> Let me upright be.

Several years later in Japan, I was invited to a picnic with a large group of Japanese school girls who were members of Y.W.C.A. clubs. In beautiful woods on the outskirts of Tokyo, we ate with chop sticks a picnic supper from little wooden boxes. Later the girls built a bonfire, with faggots they had purchased *en route*. Gathered around it in the firelight, they sang their favourite songs as young folks do in any land. Finally the young leader of the group said, "Before we leave our fire, we want to sing for our guest from Canada something we especially love." Standing in a circle under the towering trees, they sang the camp hymn in English. Never have I heard it sung more beautifully. It brought tears to my eyes. Later I asked what word had been used in the Japanese translation for "pine tree", since the pine of Japan is a crooked tree. The word used was "Tsugi", which means cryptomeria, tall and straight, like the Douglas fir of our western coast.

A most interesting translation came from Angola in Portuguese West Africa, along with an original tune and a photograph showing a large circle of African boys and girls in a jungle setting of tropical trees, presumably enjoying a sing-song.

How far a little song can travel! And how thrilling it is to realize that this little prayer of the out-of-doors is now being sung by boys and girls of many lands around the world.

*Camp Hymn**

God, Who touchest Earth with beauty,
    Make me lovely too,
With Thy Spirit re-create me,
    Make my heart anew.

Like Thy springs and running waters
    Make me crystal pure.
Like Thy rocks of towering grandeur
    Make me strong and sure.

Like Thy dancing waves in sunlight
    Make me glad and free,
Like the straightness of the pine trees
    Let me upright be.

Like the arching of the heavens
    Lift my thoughts above.
Turn my dreams to noble action,—
    Ministries of love.

God, Who touchest Earth with beauty,
    Make me lovely too,
Keep me ever, by Thy Spirit,
    Pure, and strong and true.

* See page 169 for music.

A GIFT TO AN EMPEROR

Graciousness can open doors
For which there are no keys.

THIS motto I learned while visiting in Japan. Over
and over again I experienced there a courtesy which
opened my heart to the gentle gracious women of Japan.
Illustrating this inborn sense of courtesy is the story of
a road that is famous in Japanese history. On a hiking
trip with a group of girls from the Tokyo Y.W.C.A., we
explored the Fuji Lake district. After following a narrow mountain trail for hours, we came suddenly out on
to the most beautiful road one could find anywhere.
Giant cryptomeria trees lined the roadway on either side
as far as one could see, and formed a dim arch high overhead. As we rested, before continuing our hike, Kato
San told this old tale of the Tokaido Road.

In feudal days the Emperor lived in the city of Kyoto.
Once a year from all the scattered provinces, the Daimyo,
or overlords, were required to travel to the capital to
pay homage to the Emperor. So gorgeous were these
annual processions and so great the number of retainers

that the terrific cost was reported to be a precautionary measure against any overlord accumulating enough wealth for armed revolt. Particularly spectacular were the processions from Yedo (the old name for Tokyo) and many old prints show picturesque scenes at the various inns *en route*, where the Daimyo and his retinue stayed over night. It was customary on this occasion to present a costly gift to the Emperor as a pledge of loyalty.

Now it happened that in a seaside province near Yedo there had been a terrible earthquake. Death and destruction had been augmented by fire and a tidal wave. All the people, rich and poor, had suffered greatly and there was dire need for even the barest necessities. The time came for the Daimyo of that province to make the journey to Kyoto, but he was deeply troubled. There was no gift he could take which seemed worthy of the Emperor, nor could he afford to be accompanied by any retainers. At first he thought he should forgo the journey, but this, he felt, would be to dishonour the Emperor. After much deliberation, he decided to go alone. As a gift he would present the only thing of value left in his fire-stricken province,—seeds of the cryptomeria tree, which his stout-hearted people were already beginning to plant.

Costly were the gifts presented to the Emperor: hand-painted porcelains, gold-woven brocades, richly-enameled vases, and inlaid bronze work. But when the Daimyo from the devastated province arrived, alone and on foot,

132

with his simple wooden box of seeds, the Emperor accepted it with much graciousness, as though it were the greatest gift of all. And indeed it proved to be, for the Emperor proclaimed: "A roadway shall be built from the capital city of Kyoto to Yedo, and the far-off shattered province by the sea, and it shall be lined with cryptomeria trees." Thus it came about that the famous Tokaido Road, with its avenue of giant cryptomeria trees, is still, after long centuries, the most beautiful road in all Japan.

But courtesy is not something which flourishes only on foreign soil. It flowers here and now, in our own work-a-day world and in surprising and unexpected places. One of the most gracious women I ever knew told me of visiting once in a home where an egg was served for breakfast which was "high". "I ate it," she said, "rather than embarrass my hostess." It was the same lovely person who remarked once, "To be able to overlook a neighbour's broken fence, and see only the roses that tumble over the wall, implies a very special kind of vision." There is an innate sense of human dignity and pride which often is hurt by insensitive charity and crushed by obvious sympathy. But all about us, if we are discerning, we will glimpse deep human needs that call for the gentle touch of courtesy and graciousness. This discernment is a rare art, worth a life time's learning, for it implies "a very special kind of vision", and a very understanding sort of person.

All Goodly Things

Graciousness will open wide
    The door which has no key:
The friendly smile and the gentle touch
    Are "Open, sesame!"

Courtesy weighs not the cost,
    Nor lavish gift demands;
Glimpses not the price tag,
    But open, outstretched hands.

Chivalry defends the bridge,
    With neither sword nor shield.
Battling for the wronged and weak
    No postern gate will yield.

Gallantry salutes defeat,
    Rises to fight again,
Battered but not beaten
    High triumph to attain.

All goodly things,—to be inscribed
    On an escutcheon fair,
Symbols of true nobility
    A humble heart may wear.

A JAIPUR RUG

THE Indian city of Jaipur is famous, among other things, for its beautiful hand-woven rugs of exquisite design and colour, and my parents had entered Jaipur rugs as a *must* on their shopping list. Consequently, the time came, on our tour of India, to visit that most interesting city. An unexpected letter of introduction to the Maharajah of Jaipur made the expedition doubly alluring. The letter was written by the Honourable Florence Macnaughton of the Kangra Mission Hospital. Some years earlier she had rendered noble service in that native state during a cholera epidemic and had won the lasting gratitude of the Maharajah.

In great excitement we presented ourselves at the gates of the Maharajah's palace with our precious letter, and were duly ushered into the presence of a resplendent and important looking person called the Vizier. From that moment hospitality beyond anything we could have imagined was extended to us. We were taken into the beautiful Oriental gardens where the flowers were a riot of colour, and where numerous peacocks spread their blue-green tails over the white marble balustrades. We

visited the marble-tiled pool where the Maharajah's croco-
diles were fed for our entertainment and saw the great
beds of lotus blossoms with their lovely waxen petals.
Ensconced on an elephant under a richly-embroidered
canopy, we were transported to the ancient ruined city of
Amber, several miles from the city of Jaipur, to visit the
old palace. All in all it was an experience that suggested
an Arabian Nights' entertainment. When at last we
were leaving, we were again presented to the resplendent
Vizier and my father asked him to convey to the Maharajah our most grateful thanks for the hospitality we had
enjoyed. Bowing solemnly, and without any sign of
there being anything out of the ordinary, he said, "Our
noble Maharajah, to whom your letter is addressed, died
five years ago." Such is the courtesy of the East!

Then we went shopping. What a contrast between
the peaceful landscaped gardens and the noisy crowded
bazaar! Through a maze of narrow streets we were
guided to the drab ugly sheds where the rug-makers ply
their trade. First we were taken to an office where the
beautiful rugs were unrolled for inspection. We were
then permitted to go out into the rear work sheds where
the huge looms hung from the ceiling. Seated on the
hard mud floor were hundreds of workers, boys and girls,
adults and very small children, all busily working at the
looms. Beside each one of them was a low, flat basket
filled with short pieces of wool of many colours. Their

136

fingers, as fast as they could move, were sorting and knotting the bits of wool. I wondered how they could possibly know what colours to choose, for they could not see more than a few inches of the great design. My attention was then directed to an overseer in a small balcony high up on the wall above the loom. In his hands he held the pattern and was calling out to the workers the colours they were to weave into the design. From his elevated position, he could see the rich finished pattern of the rug with its gorgeous colours of gold and blue and scarlet, and the dark tones of purple and black.

Often that visit to Jaipur flashes back in memory. But the picture that comes most frequently to mind is of the row of people seated on a mud floor weaving their bits of bright and dark wool into a design which they, themselves, could not see. It seems so like a parable of life. We, too, are called to weave into the pattern of our lives many colours. Often the colours are bright and gay, but for everyone there come times when threads of purple or black must be woven in. Not understanding, we cry out, in disappointment or sorrow, "Why must it be?" It has always helped me to remember there is One who sees the pattern as a whole, and who understands that without the dark threads there could be no rich and beautiful design. This realization helps one, when baffled and bewildered, to say, "Nevertheless, not my will, but Thine be done."

The Rug Weaver

Among the treasures garnered from the years,
   I needs must keep forever in my heart,
One vivid picture, to dispel my fears,
   And in their stead, a quiet faith impart.

      Little rug weaver I watch you,
         At work, in a far-away land,
      Where the web of the loom is before you
         And the colours lie close at your hand.
      Swiftly your fingers are knotting
         The yarns in unbroken line,
      Gold, or scarlet, or sombre shades
         In an intricate strange design.

      For you, an inscrutable canvas,
         Yet swiftly your fingers fly,
      Sure that the master-craftsman
         Directing you from on high,
      Knows when the black is needed
         Or a touch of flaming red,
      For the richness of a priceless rug
         Depends on the shades of thread.

So, like the weaver in that Eastern land,
   For whom the perfect pattern is obscure,
E'en though I ne'er completely understand,
   God help me keep my faith serene and sure.

THE IMMORTAL VIOLIN

CREMONA, in the fertile valley of the river Po in Italy, will ever be famous as the birthplace of the finest violins in all the world. The first renowned violin maker of Cremona was Andrea Amati, followed by his son Niccolo, and the latter's most brilliant and painstaking pupil, Antonio Stradivarius.

Antonio was only ten or eleven years old when he began his apprenticeship under the exacting eye of his master. While other boys of his age played in the streets of Cremona, or went on excursions to the hills, Antonio trudged off happily every morning to the workshop in the shadow of the old church. He loved to feel the smoothness of the well-seasoned pine and maple under his fingers, and to see the beautiful grain of the wood emerge, with his persistent polishing. He was fascinated by the various pieces and parts, sixty-eight or seventy, which combine to make the instrument. How very proud he was when, at the age of thirteen, he had put together all those pieces himself and had created his first violin.

For almost fourteen years Antonio served his apprenticeship. At the age of twenty-four he married and set up his own home and workshop within a stone's throw of the Amati shop. Until he was ninety-three Antonio Stradivarius worked at the craft to which he had consecrated his life. He produced about eleven hundred instruments nearly half of which have been lost in the past two centuries. Today a Stradivarius violin is almost priceless.

A story is told of Fritz Kreisler, who was browsing among old violins in an Antwerp shop. Impulsively removing his own violin from its case, he asked the dealer if he would like to buy it. The dealer promptly hailed a policeman. "Arrest this man," he said. "He is trying to sell Fritz Kreisler's violin, the Stradivarius." Without avail did Kreisler protest that he was indeed *Kreisler*; as bad luck would have it, he had no means of identification. However, he placed the precious violin beneath his chin and began to play, whereupon the astonished shopkeeper exclaimed, "Why it *is* Fritz Kreisler, and the immortal violin!"

The perfection of these violins did not happen by accident. It was painstaking effort and an exalted pride in good craftsmanship that resulted in violins that defy description or comparison.

> God be praised,
> Antonio Stradivaria has an eye
> That winces at false work and loves the true . . .
> . . . when any master hold,

'Twixt chin and hand a violin of mine,
He will be glad that Stradivaria lived,
Made violins, and made them of the best.
The masters only know whose work is good:
They will choose mine, and while God gives them skill,
I give instruments to play upon,
God choosing me to help Him . . .
        . . . if my hand slacked
I should rob God. . . .
I say, not God Himself can make man's best
Without best men to help Him.[1]

To have an exacting standard for oneself "as a workman that needeth not to be ashamed" is the challenge that comes to us from this craftsman. It is a startling thought to realize that in giving less than one's best to our particular job, we rob God and our fellow-men of something which only we could give. Work is glorified and the dedication of one's gifts—"the best of each for the good of all"—is the inspiration that comes to us from Antonio Stradivarius.

Strike true thy notes in God's great symphony.
What matters if they make but minor chord.
Not thine to say how thou shalt draw life's soul
From out the strings, but thine to keep in tune
The instrument entrusted to thy care.
To keep thy fingers firm upon the bow,
Ready to strike those notes which only thou
    Of all the universe can'st strike aright.

[1] George Eliot, "Stradivarius".

Our Task

We may not lead the orchestra,
　　Nor play first violin,
Nor see our name high-lighted
　　Upon the silver screen.
Ours may not be the picture
　　Within the gallery hung,
Nor may we write the song hit
　　To be by millions sung.

But if we do our special job
　　In an extra special way,
The inner satisfaction
　　Will immeasurably repay.
For honest effort in a task
　　Its own reward will show,
Though we win no shiny medal,
　　Deep within a pride will glow.

For each of us inherits
　　A gift that is our own,
And the world will be the poorer
　　If our work is left undone.
May we have a vision,
　　And a purpose strong and true,
To be a worthy craftsman,
　　In the work that's ours to do.

EMBROIDERED SLIPPERS

AN amazing property cupboard at camp intrigues the campers, with its varied contributions from many attics, voluminous costumes of the gay nineties, and the latest abbreviations from skating carnivals. A special property box in my cabin contains more interesting costumes from many countries; a blue crepe kimono and rice-straw sandals from Japan, a silk sari, a Mohammedan "bourka" and gold embroidered shoes from India, and a richly embroidered Mandarin coat and rose-satin slippers from China. Whenever I delve into this treasure chest, the rose-coloured slippers always bring a lump to my throat. They were a gift from a rickshaw boy in China.

In the early autumn of 1929, a friend and I bought tickets for the Orient,—destination, Peking. After short visits in Hawaii, Japan, Korea, and a hectic trip through bandit-infested Manchuria, early one November morning we looked through train windows at a strange, unfamiliar sight. A long train of heavily-laden camels was plodding along a road outside a high stone wall. We had finally reached the outskirts of the ancient city of Cathay.

For six weeks crammed with adventures, we explored the incomparable city of Peking. We learned on arrival that it was essential to engage our own rickshaw boys. Consequently, two strong Chinese lads, Number Eleven and Number Seventeen, presented themselves on the first morning with their black-lacquered, rubber-tired rickshaws. Henceforth, they took complete charge of all our comings and goings. Both were equally clean, considerate, and alert. When we stepped out of the gateway of the walled garden every morning, it was a joy to find them there, waiting to take us on our journeys of exploration. Riding in a rickshaw with Eleven holding the shafts and keeping up a steady trot was exciting enough, but added to that was the daily thrill of Peking's narrow, crowded streets with their constant pageant of colour, funeral and wedding processions, curb-side barbers and cooks, trains of laden camels, and innumerable coolies balancing great bundles on poles across their shoulders.

Eleven and Seventeen knew all the shopping streets, Silver Street, Lantern Street, Embroidery Street, etc., where we could watch the skilled craftsmen at work. They even knew which were the most honest shop-keepers on each street, and in pidgin English instructed us in the game of bartering. Tirelessly they ran with our rickshaws to all the famous places, the Temple of Confucius, the Forbidden City, with its numerous pavillions, marble bridges and palaces,—even far outside the great

144

walls of Peking to the marvellous Temple of Heaven.

One day, while we were sightseeing, a terrible sand storm blew up suddenly. Hurriedly the boys fastened the canvas top and side covers around us and bent almost double in their efforts to make headway against the blinding storm of yellow sand. I could see dimly through a tiny square of glass and the view was frightening. The wind carried dust and gravel in waves and bent the trees almost to the ground; the cloth shop signs were torn to ribbons and the red-lacquered arches were blotted out. My friend, sometimes given to exaggeration, declared, "It lifted the camels off their feet." The gritty sand penetrated the covered rickshaw, filling our nostrils and mouths. Eleven and Seventeen plodded heroically on. When at last we reached our gateway, the faces of the boys were yellow masks with only tiny slits for eyes and mouth. They grinned bravely as they helped us out of the rickshaws. We felt that a cumshaw or tip was a poor substitute for the medals they deserved.

A strange experience it was, the morning before Christmas, to be doing our Christmas shopping in the great covered market where the aisles were crowded with Chinese shoppers. We were looking for suitable gifts for Eleven and Seventeen and their families, for we had discovered each of them had a wife and child. With the gaily-wrapped parcels we had bought for them, the boys rickshawed us to a small mud-brick cottage on the

145

outskirts of the city. The two young wives were waiting for us at Eleven's house, with their adorable babies all decked out in festive red clothes. While the two-year-olds played happily with their new toys, the boys endeavoured to translate for us in their funny broken English. Our attempts to understand each other were most amusing. It was one of the happiest of all my Christmas memories.

The following July, a surprising parcel arrived at camp from far-off Peking. The parcel contained a pair of rose-satin embroidered slippers. Inside was a letter from the secretary of the Peking Y.W.C.A., in which she wrote: "Your rickshaw boy brought me this pair of slippers which his wife had embroidered for you. He did not know how to send them, but he gave me money for the postage, and I promised to mail them to you. These rickshaw boys do not often experience kindness, for theirs is a hard and bitter lot. There is a saying in China, 'The rickshaw boy sells the greatest strength and gets the smallest recompense.' Consequently, your kindness was unexpected and his sincere expression of gratitude touches me deeply." Now you will understand why a lump comes to my throat every time I come across those embroidered slippers.

So small a thing was our appreciation of faithful service, but so heart-stirring was the response of that poor Chinese rickshaw boy and his young wife. An incident such as that impresses upon us the fact that we are debtors to the known and unknown people who serve us in the routine of every-day life,—the milkman, the post-man, the street car conductor, the news boy and countless others. In the elevator of a large office building, I once asked the elevator boy if he happened to know whether Miss A. had left the building, then added, "But perhaps you do not know her!" "Of course I do!" he said en-thusiastically. "She always says 'Good Morning' to me!" Consideration and thoughtfulness are extremely impor-tant in every relationship. It is essential that we learn to treat as individuals everyone with whom we come in contact. This is fundamental Christianity.

> All service ranks the same with God. . . .
> Say not "a small event"! Why "small"?
> Costs it more pain that this, ye call
> "A great event" should come to pass,
> Than that?[1]

> I shall not pass this way again;
> Then let me now relieve some pain,
> Remove some barrier from the road,
> Or lighten someone's heavy load;
> A helping hand to this one lend,
> Then turn some other to befriend,
>   Then, O, one day
>   May someone say—
> Remembering a lessened pain,—
> "Would she could pass this way again."[2]

[1] Robert Browning, "Pippa Passes".
[2] E. R. York

147

Debtors

Debtors we are to those who serve our need,
    In all the common things of every day,
Known and unknown, of every class and creed,
    But how can we this debt outstanding pay?

Oft times in coin, and tangible reward,
    But surely we are miserly indeed
If in our hearts our generous thoughts we hoard,
    Nor pour them forth in kindly word and deed.

For work well done deserves its meed of praise,
    And are we not the poorer who withhold
The precious coin, which gratitude displays,
    From those who give us service manifold.

PATHWAYS OF LIGHT

ONE of the experiences of camp life which no camper should miss, is to paddle up the broad, silver pathway of the moonlight on a beautiful summer night. Canoeing has always seemed the poetry of motion, and, when the setting is a clear, northern night with pointed spruce and pine trees etched darkly against the sky, this is indeed a treasure to keep in one's memory book. Robert Louis Stevenson has written, "God gave us memories, that we might have roses in December," and, one might add, among many other lovely things, a paddle in the moonlight.

Every summer when the moon is "just right", we have a surprise party. We call it a "Blue Moon Night".

> Come, choose an adventure;
>   I'll grant you a boon.
> For once in the summer,
>   There'll be a "blue moon"!

Once, as we paddled back to camp after a bonfire on the opposite shore, the canoes were dotted over a fairly wide area. A camper in our canoe remarked that we were directly in the centre of the shining pathway. Then she

149

called to the other canoes which seemed to be off in the darkness, "Why don't you come over this way? We're right in the path of the moon!" Laughter came from the occupants of the other canoes, and they shouted back, "Why don't you come over this way? The light is coming straight to us!" After a friendly argument, we finally realized that none of us were in darkness, for there was a direct stream of light coming to each canoe.

The light of God's love is like that, a wide-spreading flood of light, encompassing all the races of men, yet narrowing to a single beam to reach the heart of each individual. "There is a light which lighteth every man that cometh into the world." This is our pathway of light. Could we realize what it would mean to have this gleam from the Source of all Light, available at all times, we would understand more clearly the meaning of prayer. We would see the right way more clearly and make fewer mistakes. We would go forward with greater confidence to face the baffling decisions and the unknown future. In our moment of need, light will be given to us.

> Lead, kindly light, amid the encircling gloom
>   Lead Thou me on;
> The night is dark, and I am far from home,
>   Lead Thou me on.
> Keep Thou my feet; I do not ask to see
> The distant scene; one step enough for me.[1]

[1] J. H. Newman

"Follow the Gleam" is a camp song loved by campers.

> To the knights in the days of old,
> Keeping watch on the mountain heights,
> Came a vision of Holy Grail
> And a voice through the silent night.
>
> Follow, follow, follow the gleam
> Standards of worth, o'er all the earth.
> Follow, follow, follow the gleam
> Of the light that shall bring the dawn.[1]

Each of us must try to follow the gleam of light which God gives to us. Then we, in turn, are commissioned by Jesus to let our light shine forth, that our cheerfulness and faith and courage may help others along the way and glorify our Father, the Light of the world.

Many camps close with a Vesper Service in which the campers carry forth a small lighted candle as a symbol of the light each will carry out into her wider world.

> Tiny it is,—a little taper light;
>   Frail as a dream.
> God help us keep it ever true and white,
>   A guiding gleam.

Also they sing a new verse to their song:

> And we as our camp days close,
>   Keeping our flame alight,
> Would climb where life's pathway goes,
>   Standing for truth and right.

[1] By kind permission of the Estate of the author, Sallie Hume Douglas.

151

Follow, follow, follow the gleam
    Giving our best, to meet every test,
Follow, follow, follow the gleam,
    Our best for the good of all.

Light

The moonlight makes a shining path
    As wide as the widest sea,
Yet the tiniest ship is in focus
    On the ocean's immensity.
Direct and clear as a beacon
    The light comes straight and free.

How can one doubt the sufficiency
    Of God's abounding light,
Streaming forth to all mankind,
    In a radiance infinite;
Yet coming direct to each separate craft,
    To guide its course aright.

CAMP HYMNS AND PRAYERS

An Evening Litany

Ere this day at camp be done,
Happy days of health and fun,
We give thanks at set of sun.

Thanks, O God, we give to Thee,
For Thy gifts so rich and free,
Beauty offered lavishly.

For the days of sheer delight,
Waters lit with sparkling light,
For the moon and stars at night.

For the wealth our friendships hold,
Far beyond the wealth of gold,
Richer still as we grow old,

For our homes where love is found,
Love encircling us around,
Where the joys of peace abound.

God, we offer unto Thee
Heartfelt praises full and free,
Hear our evening Litany.

Hymn of Thanks

We turn to Thee, O God, this day
    And lift our hearts anew,
To thank Thee for the loving way
    Thy care hath led us through.

For morning sun and shining dew,
    For meadows bright with flowers,
For songs of birds and waters blue,
    For clouds and gentle showers.

For dusk and rosy sunset skies,
    For twinkling stars of light,
For glowing tongues of flame that rise
    From friendly fires at night.

For comradeship and kindly mirth,
    For hearts that give us love,
For high and noble things of earth,
    That lift our thoughts above.

For simple child-like trust in Thee,
    For faith to find Thee near,
For eyes Thy wondrous works to see
    And ears Thy voice to hear.

For Thy best gift of love to earth—
    The gracious, serving One,
Who gave Himself to all the world,
    Thine own most precious Son.

Northland

Tune: "Danny Boy"

O God, our Father, who art all omnipotent,
  We bow to Thee in reverence and in praise,
With hearts that hold great gladness for Thy mercies,
  And souls that feel refreshed by wondrous days.
And God, our Father, here up in the Northland
  We feel Thy presence always very near.
We give to Thee our hands, our hearts, our voices,
  And lives, to use in faithful service unto Thee.

O Holy One, we hear Thee in all nature,
  A clarion call that bids our souls, "Awake",
The answer comes: "O Master, we are ready
  To do and give our all for Thy dear Sake!"
And when at last our lamp of life grows dimmer,
  Our day grows short, the journey almost done,
It is our prayer, our lives may hold a radiance
  As wondrous as the afterglow of sun.

Helen Ferguson Hastings

Father, Guide Us

Tune: "Pleyel", by Ignaz Joseph Pleyel

Father, guide us through this day;
May we know its gifts are Thine;
May we learn along the way
That the simple is divine.

159

May we as the morning clears
Catch its colours in our sight,
Hear its sounds with listening ears,
Touch the grasses with delight;

Feel the wind fresh from the hill,
Know the thrill of white-caps high,
Scent the depth of forests still,
Trace light clouds across the sky;

Swim with joy in waters cool,
Guide canoes as paddles gleam,
Wander by a silent pool,
Hear the laughter of a stream.

So defend us through the day
In the beauty of Thy care,
That our souls may richly say,
We have found Thee everywhere.

Mary L. Northway

Hymn of Thanksgiving

Tune: "Netherlands Folk Song", arr. by F. C. Silvester[1]

We praise Thee our Father! Oh, hear our thanksgiving
For days rich with beauty, with joy and delight;
For sunlight at noonday, the blue tint of evening,
The clear star at dusk, the quietness of night.

[1] Canadian Music Sales, Toronto.

In musical phrases Thy world offers worship:
The song of the stars and the psalm of the rain;
The wind's strong crescendo, the rush of mighty waters
All magnify Thee in resounding refrain.

The heavens adore Thee; the earth sings Thy glory
And echo the theme that the first stars began;
Oh, let all the nations rejoice now in the chorus
And sound in Thy symphony praises of man.

Mary L. Northway

For an Out-door Chapel

Tune: "The Children's Prayer", from *Hansel and Gretel*

Bless this chapel, Lord, we pray,
Keep it lovely night and day.
Bless these trees so straight and tall
Spreading sheltering arms o'er all;
Bless the sun whose friendly rays
Bid us lift our hearts in praise;
Bless the birds that sing above
Telling of the Father's love.

Bless this out-door chapel, Lord,
May we listen for Thy word.
Guide us on the upward way;
Keep us faithful day by day.
Bless us in Thy open air,
As we lift to Thee our prayer;
Now and in the years to be
Keep us ever true to Thee.

A Prayer for Camp Leaders

Lord of Creation and Author of all things true and beautiful, we humbly lift our hearts in gratitude for the wonder of Thy world, and for eyes to see the pageantry of days and nights and changing seasons. We thank Thee for the adventure and responsibility of leadership among children in their holiday time. Since Thou art the source of all wisdom, we seek to draw from Thy limitless resources, lest we fail in our task.

Take from us a false sense of our own sufficiency. Deepen our awareness of Thy all-pervading Presence about us and within us, so that at all times we may have poise, confidence, understanding and a sense of humour.

Grant that we may pass on to our campers the best Thou canst give to them through the medium of our relationship. Make us instruments worthy of the opportunity which lies before us. May we see with them, the wonder of each new day, feel their joyous zest for living, and grasp in our minds the amazing potentiality of each young life.

Help us in our camps to build bridges of friendship and understanding between our campers and peoples of different races and creeds, so that we, together, may play our part in building a better world for Thy great family of mankind.

Amen

A Camp Prayer

O Thou, who art the Father of us all, help us to realize that Thou art also the source of all power, all beauty, and all love. Help us to believe, though we may never fully understand, that all Thy resources are available for us if we have faith and dependence on Thee. Grant that we may turn to Thee humbly and expectantly in all our needs. May we be conscious of Thy nearness to us, conscious of Thy Spirit permeating all life, ever creating and ever renewing.

As we worship Thee here in the beauty of Thy out-of-doors, so may we also worship Thee when we go from this place, in our separate homes, in the crowded cities, in our various churches. Help us to realize that whenever or wherever our spirits reach out to Thee, Thou are always there.

Grant that we may face life courageously and eagerly,— with courage to meet the temptations and difficulties, also the suffering and sorrow,—and with eagerness to play our part worthily at all times.

Amen

A Camp Prayer

O loving Father of us all, we worship Thee under Thy open skies. We thank Thee that no roofs can ever shut Thee out, nor can any walls ever close Thee in, for Thou art a Spirit and abidest everywhere in Thy world. No place, however beautiful, can in itself make worship acceptable to Thee. We thank Thee, that wherever joy or gratitude, sorrow or need draw us to Thee, there is the holy place of worship.

163

Here in a world of beauty, open our eyes to see Thee in the noiseless power of growing things. Open our ears to hear Thee in the sounds and silences of shores and woods. Touch our dull hearts that we may feel Thee in the pulsing life of Thy manifold creations. Fill our hearts with quiet strength and high resolves that in Thy out-of-doors we may grow in wisdom and stature, in knowledge of Thee and in love of our fellow men.

Amen

A Prayer

O God, our Father, grant that we
May grow in grace and come to be:

Open-eyed, with a sense of wonder,
In the presence of Thy manifold beauty;

Imbued with a sense of need,
In the knowledge of Thy cleansing purity;

Inspired with a spirit of courage,
In the realization of Thy steadfastness;

Filled with a spirit of joyousness,
In the lavish sharing of Thy gifts;

Challenged with a will to honesty,
In the certainty of Thine infallible Truth;

Humbled with a sense of divine purpose,
In the astounding awareness of Thy partnership.

So shall Thy grace on us descend,—
Thy benediction, till Life's end.

A Morning Litany for Camp

For this new day, blue sky and gold of sun,
For growth upsurging from each flower and tree,
For ecstasy of morning just begun,
In glowing health and strength, with friends and fun,
    Our thanks, O God, to Thee.

For clean cool winds and balsam-scented air,
For waters gently rippled by the breeze,
For artistry and beauty everywhere,
To stir our listless hearts awake—aware,
    Our thanks we give for these.

For every winding trail we may explore,
To find adventure in the shadowed wood,
For curve of beach and lure of rocky shore,
For sense of wonder deepening more and more,
    We offer gratitude.

For all the promise of the days to be,
Glad days of summer in the open air,
For rain—the boon of every thirsty tree,
For stars that deck the night with mystery,
    For these—a fervent prayer.

For every miracle these joyous days reveal,
For growing faith in things we cannot see,
For every flash of truth we come to feel,
Which makes the meaning of all life more real,
    Our thanks O God, to Thee.

A Prayer for Out-of-Doors

We thank Thee, O Thou maker and giver of all things beautiful and good, for the vastness and the wonder of the world Thou hast created, for the beauty of lake and sky, for the delight of the eye in the colour and variety of flowers, for the ripple and music of waves and winds, for the gladness in the songs of birds, for the scent of evergreens and the refreshing touch of water. Help us, O God, lest we forget at any time whence these good things come. Fill us with the gratitude that gives thanks, not only in words, but in lives that are honest and pure and helpful.

Amen

God give me sympathy and sense
    And help me keep my courage high;
God give me calm and confidence,
    And please, a twinkle in my eye.

Benediction

Deep peace of the shining stars to you:
Deep peace of the flowing air to you:
Deep peace of the running wave to you:
Deep peace of the quiet earth to you:
Deep peace of the Prince of Peace to you:

Amen.

Fiona McLeod

A Closing Vesper Prayer

O God our Father, at this vesper hour in our out-door chapel, we gather together to give thanks unto Thee. Under Thy open skies, we would express our gratitude for the happy summer days we have spent together. We thank Thee for the friends we have made, for the beauty we have shared, and for the lessons we have learned. Grant that we may take with us, wherever we may go, the strength and steadfastness of rocks, the purity of springs and running waters, the joy and gladness of sparkling lakes, the straight uprightness of the pine trees, and in all our dreams and high resolves, give to us the high uplift of Thy arching skies. These things we ask of Thee, Great Spirit and Father of us all.

Amen

A Prayer for the Close of Camp

O God of infinite wisdom, Creator of the vast planetary system and of every tiny flower, we bow before Thee, in reverence and awe. We cannot comprehend the mysteries of Thy creation, but we believe that every shining star and every growing plant fulfils its purpose. We alone of all Thy manifold creations have the will to do, or not to do, Thy bidding. May we know Thy purpose for us, and may we earnestly endeavour to make our wills Thine own. Prepare us for the tasks that await us in Life and give us vision and courage to "follow the gleam" and to find in Thee the Light which we constantly need for ourselves, and to share with others.

Amen

167

CAMP HYMN

GLEN BERNARD.

JAMES EDMUND JONES, 1925.

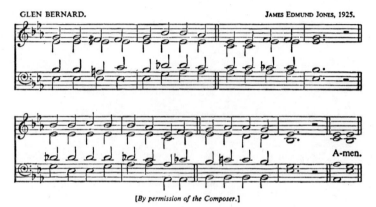

[By permission of the Composer.]

God, who touchest earth with beauty,
    Make my heart anew;
With Thy Spirit re-create me,
    Pure, and strong, and true.

God, who touchest earth with beauty,
    Make my heart anew;
Keep me ever by Thy Spirit,
    Pure, and strong, and true.[1]

[1] These verses, which differ from those on page 130, appear in the Hymn Book of the Church of England in Canada.